Thinking Biblically
About Abortion

THINKING BIBLICALLY ABOUT ABORTION

EXPLORING SCRIPTURES CONCERNING PREBORN LIFE AND ITS SANCTITY

STEVE ROHN

SEMPER REFORMANDA BOOKS
LINCOLN CENTER, KS

Thinking Biblically About Abortion: Exploring Scriptures Concerning Preborn Life and Its Sanctity

Copyright © 2025 by Steve Rohn

Published by Semper Reformanda Books

Paperback ISBN: 979-8-218-75537-9

LCCN: 2025916635

*To all the fearful women and girls facing
unplanned pregnancies.*

*To all Christians wrestling with the issue,
seeking biblical answers.*

*To all the servants of Christ who have stood
by me defending "those who are being taken
away to death" (Proverbs 24:11).*

Contents

Preface

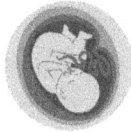

This book was born out of a desire to provide a thoroughly biblical perspective on the issue of abortion. While many pro-life resources rightly point to key verses like Psalm 139 or Luke 1, this study aims to go further.[1] While many have pointed to these passages as central to the pro-life argument, this work seeks to offer a fresh and comprehensive look at the depth of their implications within the broader context of Scripture. Though this book engages with many of the well-known texts often cited in pro-life discussions, it delves beyond surface-level arguments by exploring the fullness of Scripture's teaching on the sanctity of life and God's design for the pre-born. My goal is not merely to repeat what has been said but to build a case that is biblical, thorough, and deeply rooted in the gospel. The book also uncovers overlooked passages, makes connections between texts often considered unrelated, and builds a comprehensive biblical theology of life, human dignity, and God's compassion for the weak.

---

1   The classic proof texts and the arguments surrounding them have been recently summarized well in Wayne Grudem, *Christian Ethics: An Introduction to Biblical Moral Reasoning* (Wheaton: Crossway, 2018), 566-571. See also James K. Hoffmeier, ed., *Abortion: A Christian Understanding and Response* (Grand Rapids: Baker, 1987), 31–100; Paul B. Fowler, *Abortion: Toward an Evangelical Consensus* (Portland: Multnomah Press, 1987), 135-157.

More theological than philosophical

What makes this book unique is its singular focus on the Word of God. Rather than relying on philosophical, scientific, medical, or emotional arguments—valuable as they may be—this study centers exclusively on Scripture as the foundation for a believer's understanding of abortion and the sanctity of life. By exploring both well-known and underappreciated biblical texts, this book aims to equip Christians with a robust and faithful defense of the pro-life position.

Throughout this journey, readers will find fresh insights into passages they may have read countless times but never considered in this context. For instance, we'll explore God's intimate involvement in forming life in the womb, discover the distinction between mankind and animals, and see how ancient condemnations of child sacrifice apply to modern practices. This book connects these ideas to reveal God's heart for the preborn and His call for the church to minister in their defense.

The power of God's Word to end abortion

While many powerful arguments for the sanctity of life can be drawn from science, philosophy, and ethics,[2] this book focuses solely on the Scriptures. These other disciplines, while valuable and life-saving, are limited by human understanding and reasoning. The Bible, however, comes directly from our unchanging, all-knowing God, and as such, it holds a unique authority and power that no human argument can rival. It penetrates deeper than any scientific evidence or philosophical discourse, reaching not just the intellect but the very soul.

As Christians, our convictions must be rooted in God's revealed truth. While a mother's glimpse of her child on an ultrasound can foster a connection to the child within her, God's Word has the power to do even more. Hebrews 4:12 tells us that the Word of God is "living and active and sharper than any two-edged sword," piercing to the very

---

2   Randy Alcorn's book on the subject is phenomenal. See his *Why Pro-Life?: Caring for the Unborn and Their Mothers* (Sisters: Multnomah, 2000).

core of our being. It reveals our deepest thoughts, convicts us of sin, and opens our eyes to the gospel. In the context of abortion, Scripture provides a foundation that is unshakable because it is the eternal truth of the very Creator who forms each human life with intention and care.

By focusing on Scripture alone, this book seeks to offer Christians a foundation that transcends the shifting sands of cultural and political debates. The Word of God speaks with clarity and authority on the sanctity of life, and it alone can powerfully transform hearts and minds. Science and ethics may win arguments, but God's Word transforms hearts. This book, therefore, is not an intellectual defense of the prolife position, but a call to align our hearts with God's heart and to defend the preborn with the full conviction that comes from the declarations in His Word.

Abortion is more than a debate

Another reason this book focuses solely on God's Word is because the issue of abortion is not merely an intellectual one—it is ultimately a matter of the heart. Even if someone is presented with irrefutable evidence that life begins at conception or is persuaded by compelling ethical arguments against abortion, their heart can still rebel against God. History has shown us time and again that people are capable of ignoring what they know to be true in favor of what their unregenerate hearts desire to be true.

At its core, the abortion issue is not simply about information or education—it is about the human heart's condition before God. Scripture reveals that "the heart is more deceitful than all else" (Jer. 17:9) and that lost people, in their sinfulness, "suppress the truth in unrighteousness" (Rom. 1:18). Even when abortion is made illegal, people will often seek ways to defy the law because the root issue is not the law itself but a heart that refuses to submit to God. Abortion, like all other sins, is rooted in a rejection of God's authority and design. Until a person's heart is changed through regeneration by the Spirit of God, no amount of evidence or argument will lead to lasting transformation.

By focusing on Scripture, this book aims to do more than win debates—it seeks to reach the heart. Only the Word of God, wielded by the Spirit of God, can convict, soften, and ultimately change a heart bent on rebellion.

All objections sufficiently answered

While focusing solely on the Scriptures, this book does not set out to address many of the common questions that arise in discussions about abortion directly—questions like, "What about cases of rape or incest?" or "What if the life of the mother is at risk?" or "What about overpopulation, poverty, or unwanted children?"[3] While these are frequently debated in the public square, they are not the focus of this present work. The reason is simple: the arguments from Scripture presented in this book sufficiently answer these objections by addressing the issue of abortion *at its foundation.*

When we see from God's own testimony that the preborn are people, that He forms them with care and intention, that they are made in His image, and that He demands their protection under His Law, the objections that often distract us from the heart of the matter are swept away. These questions, though emotionally charged and rhetorically effective, do not change the reality of what God has declared about human life and its sanctity.[4]

For example, when we understand that God hates the shedding of innocent blood and views every preborn child as intrinsically valuable, it becomes clear that the circumstances of their conception or the difficulties surrounding a pregnancy cannot nullify the worth of that life. Likewise, when we see that God has consistently called His people to

---

3   For these questions, Randy Alcorn is once again extremely helpful. See his *Prolife Answers to Prochoice Arguments* (Sisters: Multnomah, 1992).

4   There must, however, be a distinction in our tone and attitude when talking with a hurting, pregnant teen who is actually living out these circumstances, as opposed to merely talking theoretically and hypothetically with an objector trying to win an argument. It is good to still have a ready answer for all of these challenging questions.

protect the vulnerable and oppressed, it follows that Christians must advocate for the preborn, no matter the challenges or objections raised.

The goal of this book, then, is to focus our attention on the truth of Scripture, which cuts through the noise of cultural arguments and debates. When we grasp what God's Word says about the sanctity of life, we are no longer swayed by questions that attempt to justify what is, at its core, the murder of innocent human beings. My hope is that by immersing ourselves in Scripture, we will gain the clarity and conviction needed to stay focused on the foundational truth: abortion ends a human life that God has created and values deeply.

Abundant grace is available

This book is written with the awareness that some readers may have deeply personal experiences with abortion—whether you have chosen it, supported someone in it, or struggled with the weight of the decision. While this book uncompromisingly proclaims the truth of God's Word about the sanctity of preborn life, it is also a message of hope. The God who forms every life in the womb is the same God who sent His Son, Jesus Christ, to redeem sinners. The Scriptures do not only reveal God's holiness and justice in judging murderers but also His mercy and grace that extends even to murderers (Luke 23:34; 1 Cor. 6:9-11).

If you have participated in abortion in any way, there is forgiveness available through the blood of Christ for every sin, including this one. The gospel assures us that Christ bore the punishment we deserve, and through repentance and faith in Him, you can stand fully justified before God. The Bible declares that "there is now no condemnation for those who are in Christ Jesus" (Rom. 8:1). The Bible promises, "If we confess our sins, He is faithful and righteous to forgive us our sins and to cleanse us from all unrighteousness" (1 John 1:9). God is eager and willing to extend forgiveness to any and all who come to Him by faith alone in Christ alone.

If you are a Christian grappling with guilt, remember that your sin is not greater than the grace of God available through Christ's atoning sacrifice (Rom. 5:20). The same Word that calls abortion sin also proclaims the sufficiency of Jesus' blood to redeem sinners and His right-eousness to justify the believer before God. Trust in Him, rest in His promises, come to the table empty-handed and freely receive all of God's salvific blessings in Christ.

This book is not written from a position of superiority or self-right-eousness but with a deep sense of humility before God's Word. The truths presented here are not merely the opinions of the author but the unchanging testimony of Scripture. As one sinner saved by grace, I ap-proach this topic with a reverence for God's truth and a desire to glorify Him by declaring His wisdom rather than my own. The goal is not to win an argument but to faithfully represent what God has said, trusting that His Word alone is sufficient to convict hearts, renew minds, and guide His people in righteousness.

Soli Deo Gloria
Here I stand, I can do no other, so help me God.
S.R.

-1-

God Forms Humans in the Womb

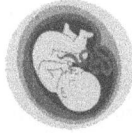

T hroughout Scripture, the act of God forming human beings in the womb is described with great detail and poetic beauty. In describing God's artistry and craftsmanship, the Scriptures often highlight not only the physical formation of our bodies but also the creation of our spirits (or souls) within us. These texts serve as the foundation for the pro-life position, emphasizing that from the earliest moments of existence, each person is the work of God's hands, intricately designed by Him. This chapter explores these crucial texts, drawing out the rich biblical doctrine of the sanctity of life and the astonishing truth that every preborn child is a unique and purposeful creation, formed by God Himself. From conception, each baby's worth and personhood is determined not by external circumstances but by their creation in God's likeness.

God's intimate and intricate creation

Psalm 139 offers a deeply personal and theological insight into God's involvement in the formation of human life in the womb. By exploring the rich language David uses to describe God's work in the womb, we gain a greater appreciation for the sanctity of life. This passage serves as a powerful affirmation of the pro-life position, emphasizing that every person, regardless of their stage of development, is "fearfully and wonderfully made" by God.

> For You formed my inward parts;
> You wove me in my mother's womb.
> I will give thanks to You, for I am fearfully and wonderfully made;
> Wonderful are Your works,
> And my soul knows it very well.
> My frame was not hidden from You,
> When I was made in secret,
> And skillfully wrought in the depths of the earth;
> Your eyes have seen my unformed substance;
> And in Your book were all written
> The days that were ordained for me,
> When as yet there was not one of them. (Psalm 139:13-16)

This text stands as a permanent testament to God's intimate involvement in the creation and development of human life in the womb. In this passage, David poetically reflects on God's meticulous care and craftsmanship in forming his entire being—body and soul.

God forms every preborn child's frame

David uses the term "frame" (v. 15) to refer to the skeletal structure or physical composition of his body.[5] This imagery emphasizes the foundational work of God in crafting the human form, highlighting that every aspect of our bodies, down to the bones, is the result of God's intentional design.

The phrase "unformed substance" (v. 16) likely refers to the embryonic stage of development. Rather than depicting a primitive understanding of biology, or referring merely to an insignificant clump of cells, David acknowledges how God was actively shaping him early

---

5   Some suggest "bones." See William L. Holladay, ed., *A Concise Hebrew and Aramaic Lexicon of the Old Testament* (Grand Rapids: Eerdmans, 1988) s.v. עֶצֶם.

in the pregnancy. This term captures the transformation from an un-recognizable form as a zygote to a fully-developed human, affirming that even at the earliest stages of gestation, we are intimately known by God, and derive our very life and existence from Him.

Every preborn child is "fearfully and wonderfully made"

The phrase "fearfully and wonderfully made" (v. 14) pairs together two picturesque words to describe the intimate care involved in God's creative work. The terms suggest a reverence and awe, indicating that during the process of forming us, God used the utmost care.

David's acknowledgment of being "fearfully and wonderfully made" serves as a testimony to the complex and delicate process of human development.

Every preborn child is made with skill

David further describes God's creative process with verbs like "formed," "wove," "made," and "skillfully wrought" (vv. 13-15). David is emphatic, piling up descriptive term after descriptive term. We cannot miss the pro-life message he is trying to drive home with this varied language.

The metaphor behind the term "formed" (v. 13a) likely suggests God's sovereign act of *gathering* all the materials needed to form a person, so to speak, much like someone acquiring the ingredients for a specific recipe, or a contractor acquiring building materials. This imagery conveys the idea of intentional design and purpose.

The next term, "wove" (v. 13b; cf. Job 10:11), gives the image of a weaver meticulously crafting a tapestry.[6] It signifies the complexity and care with which God assembles the human body, integrating every part into a cohesive whole.

---

6   Alternatively, the Hebrew word could refer to God's protection as He *covers* or *hedges in* the preborn child. Either way, the weaving metaphor is present in the word translated "skillfully wrought" (v. 15b).

After that, David acknowledges that God's work in creating life in the womb is a prime example of His "wonderful ... works" (v. 14b). David then affirms that God "made" him (v. 15a). This highlights God's creative activity, teaching us that human beings are not accidents but intentional creations of God.

Later, David says he was "skillfully wrought" (v. 15b), depicting the craftsmanship involved in human creation, likening God's work to that of a master weaver. The word is commonly used to describe the work of an embroiderer, such as the needlework and embroidery in the fabric of the tabernacle (e.g., Exod. 26:36).

All of these terms combine to describe the intricacy and precision with which God creates each individual, guiding every stage of their development in the womb. These verses collectively affirm that from the earliest stages of pregnancy, every child is fashioned with intentionality and care by a wise and mighty Creator. This understanding compels us to view every life as a valuable person worthy of protection, rather than an accident or an inconvenience.

Every preborn child has a soul

In verse 13, the term used for "inward parts" translates literally as "kidneys" (see margin). This is profoundly significant for our understanding of life in the womb. If we consider the word as a reference to the literal kidneys of David's unborn self, it serves as ancient testimony to the remarkable reality that a baby in the womb possesses all its organs very early in pregnancy. This shows how delicately and intricately God forms every part of our body—our heart, lungs, stomach, and even our intestines—during the early stages of development.[7]

Yet, a more likely interpretation, and one that carries more significance, is the metaphorical use of "kidneys" often found in the Bible. When Scripture speaks of our innards, heart, or viscera, it often speaks

---

7   Goldingay sees this as referring to physical anatomy. See John Goldingay *Psalms*, vol 3, *Psalms 90–150* (Grand Rapids: Baker Academic, 2008), 633. The Hebrew word is used of literal intestines in, for example, Exod. 29:13; Lev. 4:9; 7:4; 9:10.

to our spiritual core—our deepest emotions and soul.[8] So David might not merely be highlighting God's assembly of his *physical* body in his mother's womb, but possibly suggesting that God shaped David's very *spirit* (or soul) even before his physical birth. Therefore, he was a person with an eternal soul while still in the womb![9]

Similarly, Job 10:12 (discussed below) speaks of how his body developing in his mother also had "life" and a "spirit," indicating that his existence and essence were not merely physical, but spiritual as well.

This idea from David and Job is confirmed throughout the Bible. The prophet Zechariah proclaims how God shapes our spirits within us (Zech. 12:1; cf. Ps. 33:15; Eccl. 12:7). God is frequently referred to as "the father of spirits" (Heb. 12:9; cf. Num. 16:22; 27:16), all the way through to the closing chapter of the final book of the Canon (Rev. 22:6). Insights from Job, David, and other key passages indicate that this occurs *in utero*. In fact, Ecclesiastes 11:5 illustrates the entry of the spirit into a person's bones during gestation.[10]

God has a plan for every preborn child

In verse 16, we learn that even before David's birth, God had meticulously orchestrated all the days of his life (cf. Job 14:5). These words are not merely David's way of acknowledging God's omniscience and sovereign plan *in general*. Here, David, in acknowledging God's control of all events, *personalizes* God's ultimate plan. He believes that God's

---

8   cf. Pss. 7:9; 26:2; 73:21; Prov. 23:16; Jer. 11:20; 12:2; 17:10; 20:12. See Robert B. Chisholm, "כִּלְיָה," in ed. Willem A. VanGemeren, *New International Dictionary of Old Testament Theology and Exegesis*, vol. 2 (Grand Rapids: Zondervan, 1997), 656–57.

9   This biblical truth powerfully disproves Simmons's unfounded claim that "the fetus is not a person to the same degree or in the same sense as the woman" (Paul D. Simmons, "Abortion," in ed. Watson E. Mills, *Mercer Dictionary of the Bible* [Macon: Mercer University Press, 1990], 5).

10   This could refer to what the Bible calls the "breath of life" rather than one's eternal soul. This is still significant because the breath of life is what makes something a living being.

plan encompasses the intricate details of each individual's life, written in stone even before they are ever born.[11]

This truth is confirmed in Jeremiah 1:5, where God addresses the prophet, declaring, "Before I formed you in the womb I knew you, and before you were born I consecrated you." It is vital to note the speaker here—this is not Jeremiah's own conjecture but the declaration of God Himself, giving testimony to His intimate involvement in the plan and design of each life.

The apostle Paul understood this as well. He articulates how God "set me apart even from my mother's womb," saving him and commissioning him to preach to the Gentiles (Gal. 1:15).

These verses show us God's involvement in the lives of every preborn child. They show His meticulous care and purposeful design of not only the larger aspects of life—our vocational or ministerial calling, as in Jeremiah's and Paul's case—but the details of every minute of every day of each person's life before they are born, as in David's case.

Notice also how these passages from Jeremiah and Paul not only reinforce the scriptural affirmation of God's role in shaping life in the womb and planning their steps, but also emphasize the continuity of the person's identity both inside and outside the womb. Jeremiah remained Jeremiah ("I formed *you* in the womb," emphasis mine), and Paul remained Paul ("set *me* apart," emphasis mine). They were not someone—or some*thing*—different before and after birth.[12]

God is faithful throughout all life

We also see that the biblical authors viewed their preborn selves as the same person when we look at the central theme of Psalm 139. Why is David bringing up the formation of his preborn self in the first place?

---

11 If God's "book" that is "written" in is the same as the "book of life" frequently mentioned in Scripture, then this passage hints that the preborn are eternal souls whose eternal destinies have already been determined.

12 This staggering detail should not be overlooked. It will appear several more times in this study. See also John Stott, *Issues Facing Christians Today*, 4th ed. (Grand Rapids: Zondervan, 2006), 396–401.

David's point is God's enduring faithfulness throughout his entire life. In this Psalm, David feels confidence in God at present because of His consistent goodness toward him, even during his time in the womb. His assurance lies in the conviction that God will safeguard him now, just as He had since before he was born (cf. Ps. 71:6; Isa. 46:3-4). This intricate involvement of God in the formation of his life within the womb fuels David's trust in God's preservation of his life in the present.

This theme of trusting God in the present based on His faithfulness in the past (before birth) is exactly the same idea as in Job 10:8-12, discussed below. Job begins the passage with a rhetorical question, asking why God, who was so careful in Job's creation and formation, would suddenly turn against him (v. 8). The Hebrew word for "fashioned" in verse 8 stresses the pains God underwent to create Job. Job essentially asks God, "Since You went through so much trouble to make me, why destroy Your handiwork?"

So then, if God's faithfulness to David extends all the way back even to the intricate care he received in the womb, then David clearly views the baby in his mother's womb as the same person he is now.

Job's fetal development

This next key passage contains several elements similar to those discussed in Psalm 139. The Scriptural testimony is consistent.

Your hands fashioned and made me altogether,
And would You destroy me?
Remember now, that You have made me as clay;
And would You turn me into dust again?
Did You not pour me out like milk
And curdle me like cheese;
Clothe me with skin and flesh,
And knit me together with bones and sinews?
You have granted me life and lovingkindness;
And Your care has preserved my spirit. (Job 10:8-12)

God's creative action

In these verses, Job vividly illustrates the meticulous craftsmanship employed by God in forming his body within the womb in a similar fashion to Psalm 139. The phrases "fashioned and made" (v. 8a), "made ... as clay" (v. 9), the metaphorical references to milk and cheese (v. 10), the ideas of being "clothe[d]" with skin (v. 11a) and "knit ... together" in the womb (v. 11b) all come together to paint a vivid portrait of the intricate and deliberate process involved in shaping Job's physical and spiritual being.

Each of these important terms and phrases sheds more light on this delicate and precious process. First, that the preborn Job was "fashioned and made" suggests the deliberate crafting of every detail. Then the fact that God "made me as clay" illustrates the moldable nature of human form in the hands of God (cf. Isa. 29:16), while the illustrations of pouring out milk and curdling cheese hint at God's total control over the process. Additionally, being "clothe[d]" and "knit ... together" evoke a sense of the intricate construction of layer after layer of human anatomy from interwoven veins, capillaries, and nerves to our dermal exterior.[13]

We do not necessarily need to dwell on what exact part of fetal development each of these terms symbolizes. They simply paint a picture, pointing to the reality that there is great attention to detail behind God's creative actions.

The same Job inside and outside the womb

Notice also how Job, like other biblical authors mentioned above, consistently refers to the baby in his mother's womb as himself throughout this passage, calling his preborn self "me." Similar to David's perspec-

---

13 Note the striking similarities between this description of the formation of a preborn child here and the restoration of a dead body through miraculous resurrection in Ezek. 37: "Behold, I will cause breath to enter you that you may come to life. I will put sinews on you, make flesh grow back on you, cover you with skin and put breath in you that you may come alive" (vv. 5-6; cf. vv. 7-10).

tive, Job perceives his identity as continuous both inside and outside the womb. What God was sculpting within the womb was undeniably Job—identical to the person he was at that moment of speaking.

Job's physical and spiritual development

The bodily elements mentioned in verse 11—skin, flesh, bones, and sinews—show the physical development within Job's prenatal state. Again, all of these features are present early in the development process. Preborn Job had all the same body parts he had as a fully grown man.

Job's *spiritual* development is seen in his declaration in verse 12 that God has given him "life," as well as the explicit reference to God preserving his "spirit." This is clear biblical testimony to the fact that every preborn child is a living person, as well as a human with a soul.

As noted earlier, this passage is about Job's present trust in God's continued care based on His care in the past. So if Job believes that God will continue to preserve his spirit, that must mean Job believes that God was preserving it back while he was still in the womb, which would indicate that preborn babies have spirits.

Additionally, the encompassing nature of the term "altogether" or, in the margin, "together round about" (v. 8a) appears to extend beyond the physical body, embracing both Job's corporeal existence and the essence of his soul.[14]

Job also asks God if He would suddenly turn and destroy "me" (v. 8b). "Me" naturally includes the entire person, body and soul. This deep understanding underlines the inseparable connection between one's physical and spiritual being, and provides further evidence that the preborn have souls, being a complete human person even in the womb.

---

14 Exod. 21:22-25 protects a preborn child under the law of "life for life" (or possibly, "soul for soul"); demonstrating that the preborn are living beings (with souls). See the Appendix for further discussion of this passage.

Slave and free fashioned by God

In another insightful text, Job says:

> If I have despised the claim of my male or female slaves
> When they filed a complaint against me,
> What then could I do when God arises?
> And when He calls me to account, what will I answer Him?
> Did not He who made me in the womb make him,
> And the same one fashion us in the womb? (Job 31:13-15)

In this eye-opening passage, we encounter yet another depiction of God's intimate involvement in the creation of human life within the womb. Job echoes the language of being "made" and "fashion[ed]" by God during gestation.

Once more, Job employs the first-person pronouns—"me" and "I"—emphasizing his recognition of the baby within the womb as an inseparable part of his own identity. This continuity of personality is true of the servant as well, calling the preborn servant in the womb "him" and, both together, referring to them as "us." This reinforces the notion that these individuals were not impersonal entities transformed by a mystical passage through the birth canal but were recognized as the same individuals from conception onward.

This passage also powerfully affirms the equality of all human be-ings. Job's words establish the belief that all individuals, regardless of their socio-economic status—rich or poor, slave or free—have been meticulously fashioned by God. Consequently, this truth demands that each person be treated with fairness and impartiality.[15]

Solomon echoes this sentiment when he declares, "The rich and the poor have a common bond, the LORD is the maker of them all" (Prov.

---

15 Rather than condoning slavery, this passage provides theological grounds for prohibiting any mistreatment of those we deem inferior. Job's words support the biblical doctrine of *imago Dei*, demonstrating how a proper un-derstanding of man's origins is foundational to the discussion of equal rights for all.

22:2; cf. 14:31; 17:5; 29:13), further emphasizing the shared divine origin and intrinsic worth of every individual.

I took you from the womb

In addition to the foundational passages affirming the sanctity of life, numerous other texts emphasize the divine act of forming life within the womb. God is frequently described as being present with someone from their earliest days of gestation, watching over them, and guiding their emergence into the world.

As we delve into these verses, pay attention once more to the first-person pronouns. These pronouns embrace the entirety of the individual, encompassing both their body and soul. This recurring usage reaffirms the biblical authors' belief in the continuity of their identity, extending from pre-birth to post-birth existence.

In Isaiah 44:2, God declares Himself to be the one who "made you and formed you from the womb" (cf. v. 24).[16] Similarly, in Isaiah 46:3, God says, "you who have been borne by Me from birth[17] and have been carried from the womb."[18] Psalm 71 echoes this truth, stating, "You are He who took me from my mother's womb" (v. 6; cf. Job 1:21).[19] We see from these verses that the preborn are people whom God cares for—the same people of God *outside* the womb.

---

16 Isaiah regularly speaks of God forming people, often in the womb (Isa. 43:1, 7, 21; 44:2; 21, 24; 49:5; cf. Jer. 1:5). Some scholars connect the Hebrew term used here to Gen. 2:7, suggesting that procreation is a co-creative process between God, man, and woman. See James K. Hoffmeier *Abortion*, 56.

17 The word translated "birth" in this verse literally refers to the womb, as seen in the following passages: Gen. 25:23-24; 38:27; Deut. 7:13; 28:4, 11, 18, 53; 30:9; Judg. 13:5, 7; Job 1:21; 3:11; 10:19; 31:15; 38:29; Pss. 22:10; 58:3; 71:6; Eccl. 11:5; Isa. 44:2, 24; 48:8; 49:1, 5; Hos. 9:11, 16.

18 While these Isaiah passages address the nation of Israel, the imagery of birth is drawn from normal human experience and does not diminish the pro-life implications of the text.

19 The same truth is expressed in the prophetic words of Jesus Himself in Ps. 22:9-10 and Isa. 49:1, 5.

Moreover, in Psalm 119:73, the psalmist acknowledges, "Your hands made me and fashioned me." Solomon, in Proverbs 22:2, says that God is the Maker of both the rich and the poor, highlighting the equal rights and value of all individuals before God.

While Scripture speaks of God's creation of mankind collectively, the biblical authors discerned a more personal aspect, acknowledging God's intimate involvement in each individual's formation. By interpreting Scripture with Scripture, it becomes evident that God's work of shaping and caring for us begins not at birth but approximately nine months earlier.

The biblical witness, as examined in this chapter, emphatically teaches the sanctity of life, revealing a God who is intimately involved in the creation of each human being inside their mother's womb. From the poetic depths of Psalm 139, where David marvels at God's intricate formation of his body and soul, to the insights regarding Jeremiah and Paul, the Scriptures consistently affirm that life begins at conception and that the preborn are developed and watched over by God.

These texts collectively emphasize that every human being, regardless of their stage of development, is precious in God's eyes and fully human. This understanding compels us to honor and protect life at all stages, recognizing that our worth is derived not from our circumstances or environment but from being fearfully and wonderfully made by our Creator.

-2-

"Children" Inside
the Womb

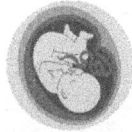

I n addition to the passages regarding God forming people in the womb discussed in the previous chapter, evidence for the humanity of the fetus can be gleaned from the Bible's consistent use of the same word for "child" both outside and inside the womb. This chapter delves into the biblical evidence to uncover the significance of this terminology, shedding light on how the Bible recognizes and affirms the personhood of the preborn.

John the Baptist and Jesus (Luke 1)

In Luke 1:41 and 44, the preborn John the Baptist is referred to as a child. This is the Greek word for a small child, used by Luke in a nearby context to refer to Jesus after His birth (2:12, 16).[20] In addition to this term, Mary is told that Elizabeth "conceived a *son* in her old age" (Luke 1:36, emphasis mine). This means that John was her son

---

20 Consider also Exod. 21:22-25, where an unborn baby harmed in a scuffle is considered a "child." See the Appendix for further discussion of this passage.

even before his birth. A woman does not need to wait to give birth before she can be called a mother!

When Elizabeth encountered Mary, her baby "leaped in her womb," expressing joy (Luke 1:41). This means that a child in the womb experiences emotions, showing they have a heart, feelings, and personality. It is evident from this biblical account that John not only exhibited human emotions in the womb but was also "filled with the Holy Spirit while yet in his mother's womb" (v. 15).[21] The Holy Spirit does not fill inanimate objects, or clumps of cells; He indwells *humans*.

It is extremely important to note the timing of this encounter. We know that John the Baptist was six months older than Jesus. So at the time of this encounter Mary must have been in her first trimester. In fact, the account even says that Mary "went in a hurry" to see Elizabeth immediately upon becoming pregnant (v. 39). Luke's mention of Mary's swift journey to Elizabeth indicates that this meeting likely occurred very early in her pregnancy. It could have even taken place when Jesus was as young as a week old! This highlights that Jesus, when He was titled "Lord" (v. 43), could have been anywhere from a first-trimester baby to a week-old zygote.

In Luke 2:21, the explicit reference to Jesus being "conceived in the womb" emphasizes the personhood of the child—the unborn baby was Jesus. The term "He" used to describe Him proves His identity as an individual, distinct person even in the womb.

Moreover, the term "fruit" (Luke 1:42), used symbolically in Scripture to denote offspring, recognizes Jesus as a living being, a continuation of the lineage of humanity through His mother.[22] The most significant aspect, however, lies in Mary being referred to as the

---

21 This instance appears to be a unique, miraculous event rather than a universal truth that all preborn children are filled with the Spirit.
22 Consider also the biblical metaphor of children as one's "seed" (often translated "descendants"). See Lev. 12:2, where a woman "produces seed" (literal translation) in the womb, or Num. 5:28, where a woman "conceives seed" (literal translation).

"mother of my [Elizabeth's] Lord" (v. 43) signifying Jesus' Lordship even in the womb!

This recognition of Christ's personhood within the virgin's womb is confirmed by Old Testament prophecies of His coming. Psalm 22, a Messianic psalm portraying the Savior's suffering, is written from the perspective of Jesus Himself. The Messianic figure expresses His trust in God "from birth" (v. 10a, literally "womb") and "from my mother's womb" (v. 10b).

Similarly, another Messianic prophecy portrays the coming Savior stating, "The LORD called Me from the womb; from the body of My mother He named Me" (Isa. 49:1). This prophecy emphasizes that God shaped and formed Jesus in the womb to serve His purpose (v. 5) and that Jesus knew the Father and worshiped Him even before birth.

Samson (Judg. 13)

In the significant passage foretelling the birth of Samson (Judg. 13), the preborn child of Manoah and his wife is explicitly referred to as a "boy,"[23] a "son," and uniquely identified as a "Nazirite." Inside his mother's womb, therefore, lived a boy who was considered one of her descendants in filial relation to her, and one who was in covenant relationship with God.

Of particular interest is how his mother is specifically instructed to abstain from wine, highlighting that Samson, even in the womb, was under the Nazirite vow already (vv. 4, 7, 14). From conception, Samson was morally obligated to uphold this sacred commitment to God. The careful instructions given to Samson's mother regarding wine consumption are not merely a dietary restriction but a crucial aspect of his relationship with God as a Nazirite.

The process of maternal-fetal nutrient transport illustrates how substances consumed by the mother can pass through the placenta and impact the developing child. In this case, had Samson's mother con-

---

23 Verses 5, 8. Literally a "child"; the same Hebrew word as in v. 24 referring to Samson *after* birth.

sumed wine, it would have caused her son to unknowingly violate his Nazirite vow before his birth.[24]

The complexity of Samson's situation challenges the notion that he was merely a non-human life form. His identification as a Nazirite—a title with such religious significance—acknowledges his personhood and individuality even in the womb.

Jacob and Esau (Gen. 25)

The account of Rebekah's pregnancy with twins (Genesis 25:19-26) offers additional compelling evidence of life within the womb. Initially, in verse 22, the two sons within her womb are unmistakably referred to as "children." Furthermore, verse 24 emphasizes that she was carrying "twins" in her womb, reinforcing the recognition of distinct human lives within her.

The Lord's revelation to Rebekah about these two children shows that within her womb resided not merely two fetuses but "two nations" and "two peoples" (v. 23). This insight into God's plan, repeated in Romans 9, displays the sovereignty of God in weaving His redemptive plan through individuals even before their birth. It is astounding to consider that God's design for our earthly and eternal destinies is set in motion while we are still in the womb (and long before!).

Also, the fulfillment of the prophecy that the older will serve the younger is demonstrated in that God loved one and hated the other (Rom. 9:13; cf. Mal. 1:2-3), showing how God has already planned the days of their lives as well as their eternal destinies before birth.[25]

We find a striking parallel in another biblical account involving twins, found later in Genesis. We are told that Tamar was carrying "twins in her womb" (Gen. 38:27), emphasizing the acknowledgment of these two entities as human beings before their birth. They are re-

---

24 One astonishing observation is that she had to do this despite not being a Nazirite herself. During pregnancy, the baby is a distinct person with a different body than the mother.

25 See also Hos. 12:3. The "he" (Jacob) who grabbed hold of his brother's heel in the womb is the same "he" who contended with God as an adult.

ferred to as each other's "brother" even before their delivery (vv. 29-30), signifying their recognition as individuals prior to their birth, as well as their relationship to other humans.[26]

I regret the day I was born

In both of the following rather gloomy passages, the speaker laments the day of their birth. Looking beyond the sorrow and emotion to their theological significance, these laments shed light on the Old Testament understanding of the personhood of the preborn. Both Job and Jeremiah refer to their preborn selves as a continuation of their own identity—the same before and after birth. It is evident that they regarded themselves as unchanged, whether inside or outside the womb. Thus, when they speak of a miscarriage, it is as if they themselves ceased to exist.

Job acknowledges his preborn self

In Job 3:11-19, Job reflects on the possibility of emerging as a stillborn from the womb, consistently using "I" to reference his preborn self. He unmistakably perceives his preborn state as himself, reinforcing the understanding that Job was Job within the womb, existing and potentially perishing as a human. This biblical portrayal of the preborn disproves the notion that unborn babies are inhuman, gaining personhood only after birth.

His desire to have died prematurely in verse 11 implies the status of the fetus as a living being—for only the living can die. The mention of other "infants that never saw light" (v. 16) describes those unfortunate children who never left the womb as *individuals*. Remarkably, Job labels

---

26 In addition to the passages above, Acts 3:2 and 14:8 mention two men who were lame from their mother's womb. While not using the term for "child," these texts affirm both the continuity of personhood before and after birth and the fact that a fetus is a human being. Lenski, in his commentary *ad loc.*, wrongly assumes that the men were injured at birth rather than lame while still inside their mothers, as the texts make clear.

them as "infants," a Hebrew term consistently used to denote small children or suckling babes.[27]

Furthermore, Job's lament contains scattered references to an after-life, implying his belief that even those in the womb possess an eternal soul.

Jeremiah's preborn personhood

In Jeremiah 20:14-18, amid his despair, the prophet expresses regret at being born. Yet, within this lament, we find rich insight into the personhood of the preborn.

> Cursed be the day when I was born;
> Let the day not be blessed when my mother bore me!
> Cursed be the man who brought the news
> To my father, saying,
> "A baby boy has been born to you!"
> And made him very happy.
> But let that man be like the cities
> Which the LORD overthrew without relenting,
> And let him hear an outcry in the morning
> And a shout of alarm at noon;
> Because he did not kill me before birth,
> So that my mother would have been my grave,
> And her womb ever pregnant.
> Why did I ever come forth from the womb
> To look on trouble and sorrow,
> So that my days have been spent in shame? (Jeremiah 20:14-18)

Jeremiah's plea in verse 17, in which he wishes someone had killed him in the womb, identifies his preborn self as "me." Particularly striking is his description of the baby inside his mother—whom he sees as himself—being "kill[ed]" (v. 17a), and having his mother as his grave (v.

---

27 Such as the children who were praising Jesus on Palm Sunday (Ps. 8:2; cf. Matt. 21:16), or in the context of women and children being tragically killed in war (1 Sam. 15:3; 22:19; 2 Kgs. 8:12; Ps. 137:9; Isa. 13:16; Jer. 44:7; Nah. 3:10). In each context, young children are in mind (cf. Ps. 17:14; Isa. 3:12; Jer. 6:11; 9:21; Lam. 1:5; 2:11, 20; 4:4; Joel 2:16; Mic. 2:9).

17b). This language raises the question: how can one "kill" something that isn't alive?

Throughout the concluding verses of this passage, Jeremiah consistently refers to his preborn self in the first person. Further, he describes himself emerging from the womb, emphasizing that no change in personhood happens during the birth process. *Jeremiah* will emerge from the womb.

Together, these passages from Job and Jeremiah testify to the understanding that a fetus is a living human person—unchanged before and after birth.

She conceived and bore a son

There is a common phrase used to describe the bearing of children throughout the Old Testament: "[She] conceived and bore a son" (Gen. 4:1, 17; 21:2; 29:32; 30:5, 17, 23; 38:3; Exod. 2:2; Judg. 13:3, 5, 7; 1 Sam. 2:21; 2 Kgs. 4:17; 1 Chr. 7:23; Isa. 8:3; Hos. 1:3, 8).[28]

In each instance, the language links the *conceiving* and the *bearing* of the children with the same object, emphasizing that what is conceived is identical to what is borne. It becomes evident that the mother does not conceive a clump of cells or an inanimate object but a human child, who is equally alive and equally human as the child to whom she gives birth.

Perhaps one may object that the wording is ambiguous, or that the idea is rather that the woman conceives—period—and also gives birth to a child later on. In this case, what is borne is a child but what is conceived remains unidentified. In response, several passages use the conception and birth process as a metaphor, where what is conceived is undeniably the same as what is borne. These clearer texts, discussed below, highlight that the biblical authors connect both verbs to the object.

For instance, consider Numbers 11:12, where Moses says to God, "Was it I who conceived all this people? Was it I who brought them

---

28   See also Gen. 16:4-5, 11; 29:33-35; 30:7, 19; 38:4; Ruth 4:13; 1 Sam. 1:20; Hos. 1:6 where more ambiguous phrases are used.

forth...?" This text clarifies any confusion in the verbiage. It reveals that according to the biblical perspective, whatever or whoever was *conceived* is the same as what or who comes forth at birth.

The account of Hannah's children after Samuel in 1 Samuel 2:21 is also helpful. We are told, "The LORD visited Hannah; and she conceived and gave birth to three sons and two daughters." Unless one suggests that Hannah had quintuplets in her first pregnancy after Samuel, the language in this verse dismisses the notion that a mother conceives an inanimate object but then gives birth to a human baby. Once more, in these phrases both verbs are attached to the noun, affirming that a human child is conceived in the womb.

This construction—where conception and birth refer to the same person—is also used metaphorically in Scripture. These other instances bring clarity to the literal birth scenarios, showing that what is conceived is the same as what is later brought forth:

> They conceive mischief and bring forth iniquity. (Job 15:35)

> He conceives mischief and brings forth falsehood. (Psalm 7:14)

> You have conceived chaff, you will give birth to stubble. (Isaiah 33:11)[29]

In this metaphorical usage, Isaiah 59:13 stands out as particularly instructive: "Conceiving in and uttering from the heart lying words" (cf. v. 4). Here, the same "lying words" conceived are what is brought forth out of the mouth. And so, if a woman gives birth to a child, a child is what she conceived; if a baby comes out of a mother it naturally follows that a baby was inside of her.

More conception terminology

Biblical authors sometimes omit mentioning birth altogether, using conception vocabulary as a sufficient substitute for the whole process.

---

29 cf. Jas. 1:15. The fact that what is conceived and what is borne is described with different words in these verses does not diminish their significance for our discussion. The difference in vocabulary does not refer to different entities; rather, the variation serves to create parallelism or, in some cases, intensification.

"Children" Inside the Womb

For instance, in 1 Chronicles 4:17, Jalon conceives Miriam, Shammai, and Ishbah. No mention is made of their births; she simply conceives her children. Once more, what was conceived was the child in each case.

Consider also the Bible passages where what is conceived is referred to as "me," indicating the author sees themselves as the same person inside the womb, or when what is conceived is referred to as a *person*, indicating that the preborn is a human being:

> In sin my mother conceived *me*. (Psalm 51:5, emphasis mine)[30]

> . . . into the room of her who conceived *me*. (Song of Solomon 3:4, emphasis mine)

> Let the day perish on which I was to be born, and the night which said, "A *boy* is conceived." (Job 3:3, emphasis mine)

> She who conceived *them* has acted shamefully. (Hosea 2:5, emphasis mine)

Thus, the inspired writers of Scripture believed that their "fetuses" were living persons—the same individuals they were at the time of writing. In every single biblical pregnancy, what is conceived in the womb is never described as anything less than a fully human child.

The exploration of Scripture in this chapter provides undeniable proof of the personhood of the preborn. They are consistently portrayed as "children" with distinct identities and God-given purposes. From the early life of figures like John the Baptist, Jesus, and Samson, to the per-

---

30 Here, and even more explicitly in Ps. 58:3, the preborn are considered moral beings who have sinned against God. This not only proves that they are more than inanimate objects but also establishes their humanity by connecting them to Adam, the head of the human race, whose sin they are guilty of (cf. Rom. 5:12-19; 1 Cor. 15:21-22). For how Ps. 51:5 relates to the preborn as a morally responsible human being, see also John Jefferson Davis, *Abortion and the Christian: What Every Believer Should Know* (Phillipsburg: Presbyterian and Reformed, 1984), 41–42, 45–46.

sonal reflections of Job and Jeremiah, the Scripture consistently ac-knowledges the preborn as full persons with value and purpose.

The consistent use of the term "child" for the preborn throughout these accounts shows the continuity of identity from the womb to the world. The preborn are not potential lives or mere biological entities but are recognized as full persons. This understanding challenges any justification for abortion, as it contradicts the biblical truth that each life is sacred and worthy of protection.

In a culture that often dehumanizes the preborn, these scriptural truths call us to be steadfast advocates for the sanctity of life, upholding the value and dignity of every person.

-3-

Mankind Distinct from Animals

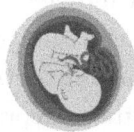

T his chapter explores the biblical doctrine that mankind is created in the image of God, as well as its implications for understanding the sanctity of human life. Unlike any other part of creation, humans bear God's image and likeness. This astounding reality means that man has a unique dignity, worth, and moral responsibility. This truth applies to each and every human being, from conception onward, affirming the intrinsic value of preborn life.[31]

In light of this unique blessing, Scripture consistently draws a sharp distinction between mankind and the animal kingdom. While animals are part of God's creation, only humans are granted the sacred privilege of being image-bearers, setting us apart in ways that demand respect, protection, and care for all human life. These theological truths provide an unshakable foundation for the pro-life position, demonstrating that preborn boys and girls share fully in the image of God and are therefore worthy of the same protection as all other human beings.

---

31 Without even mentioning the image of God in man, the mere fact that God creates a person gives them value. Moreover, the fact that all men share this same origin in God establishes their equality and worthiness of protection (Job 31:13-15; Prov. 22:2).

Made in God's image

In Genesis 1:26 God says, "Let Us make man in Our image, according to Our likeness." This is an amazing facet of our existence as humans that God did not grant to any other creature. In fact, God placed mankind *over* the rest of creation when He commanded Adam, "Be fruitful and multiply, and fill the earth, and *subdue* it; and *rule* over the fish of the sea and over the birds of the sky and over every living thing that moves on the earth" (Gen. 1:28, emphasis mine).

While we don't physically resemble God—for "God is spirit" (John 4:24)—part of the image is being His representatives on Earth. As we tread upon this planet, we stand as tangible reminders of His dominion, extending His reign simply through our very existence.[32]

The unchanging aspect of man being made in the image of God remains true, even post-fall. Biblical declarations unequivocally affirm this truth, emphasizing our intrinsic representation of God's image in texts written after the fall itself (Gen. 9:6; 1 Cor. 11:7; Jas. 3:9).[33] This permanence shows that our likeness to God, and all its implications, was not affected (at least entirely) by mankind's fall into sin and death.[34]

---

32 For an excellent treatment of the meaning of the image of God from a historical and linguistic standpoint, see Peter J. Gentry and Stephen J. Wellum, *Kingdom Through Covenant: A Biblical-Theological Understanding of the Covenants* (Wheaton: Crossway, 2012), 184–202. See also Raymond C. Van Leeuwen, "Form, Image," *NIDOTTE* 4:644–45.

33 In Jas. 3:9, the perfect tense of "made" is used, indicating that we *were* and *continue to be* in God's image. See Chris A. Vlachos, *James*, Exegetical Guide to the Greek New Testament (Nashville: B&H Academic, 2013), 115; as well as Hort's commentary on James *ad loc.*

34 Eph. 4:24 and Col. 3:10 (cf. Rom. 8:29; 2 Cor. 3:18) are often cited as evidence that the image of God in man has been marred by the fall (e.g., Anthony A. Hoekema, *Created in God's Image* [Grand Rapids: Eerdmans, 1994], 22–28). However, the renewal into Christ's image described in these verses is not merely a reversion to our original state but a transformation into something greater. "Renewal," for example, refers not to returning to an old state but being transformed into a qualitatively different (here, *better*) state.

The image of God and man's value

The doctrine that man is created in the image of God is where the rubber meets the road in the abortion debate. Herein, we truly understand the intrinsic value of every human being.[35] What defines our worth? Is it the circumstances at birth, our abilities, or our contribution to society? Is it decided by our potential, our genetics, our race, our gender?

The truth that humans are made in God's image forms the foundation of all basic human rights. It is this biblical doctrine alone that forever settles why every individual deserves equal protection under the law, particularly from heinous acts like murder.

Our value and dignity come from our Creator and cannot be stripped away by societal norms or government regulations. The image of God in humanity bestows dignity upon each person, regardless of skin color, physical stature, or dependency on their mother for sustenance and survival.

This truth finds support in passages where the sanctity of human life, marked by the image of God, is grounds for prohibiting both verbal and physical harm to mankind.

In Genesis 9, God instructs Noah about the sanctity of human life by emphasizing that anyone who sheds human blood must face the ultimate consequence. This principle of life for life is rooted in ("for") the fact that "in the image of God He made man" (v. 6), declaring human life immensely valuable and worthy of protection.[36]

---

35 Donald M. Lake, "A Theological Perspective on Abortion," in Hoffmeier, *Abortion*, 89–91; Davis, *Abortion and the Christian*, 35–40.

36 Genesis 9 answers the common objection that Christians are only partially pro-life or that they are inconsistent if they oppose abortion while supporting capital punishment. Yet in this passage, the Bible states that those who kill image-bearers are to have their own blood shed as a form of divinely sanctioned capital punishment. Clearly, then, God distinguishes between killing the innocent and punishing criminals. One can support the death penalty for murderers without compromising pro-life convictions (cf. Lev. 24:17-23; Num. 35:33). See Gerhard von Rad, *Genesis: A Commentary* (Philadelphia: Westminster, 1972), 132–33; Clifford E. Bajema, *Abortion and the Meaning of Personhood* (Grand Rapids: Baker, 1974), 53–54.

This principle is echoed in the New Testament by James. He high-lights the contradiction in our speech, where we praise the Lord yet curse fellow human beings—often in the same breath! James empha-sizes that this act of cursing someone, who is "made in the likeness of God" (Jas. 3:9), is deeply sinful. His exhortation reveals that this truth doesn't just forbid murder, as in Genesis, but extends to how we treat others with our words.

So then, man must neither be *assaulted* (Gen. 9:6) nor *insulted* (Jas. 3:9) specifically because he is made in God's image. Everyone deserves protection, not just in church but in society at large, because of this in-herent quality in each person, born or not.[37]

Psalm 8 and the image of God

Psalm 8 powerfully depicts the intrinsic value and honor humanity pos-sesses over and above the rest of creation, even without explicitly mentioning the image of God. It is a psalm that describes the dignity mankind embodies.

> When I consider Your heavens, the work of Your fingers,
> The moon and the stars, which You have ordained;
> What is man that You take thought of him,
> And the son of man that You care for him?
> Yet You have made him a little lower than God,[38]
> And You crown him with glory and majesty!
> You make him to rule over the works of Your hands;
> You have put all things under his feet,
> All sheep and oxen,
> And also the beasts of the field,
> The birds of the heavens and the fish of the sea,
> Whatever passes through the paths of the seas. (Psalm 8:3-8)

---

37 See also G. C. Berkouwer, *Man: The Image of God* (Grand Rapids: Eerd-mans, 1962), 59.

38 Or, "lower than the angels" (Heb. 2:7). See George Guthrie's discussion in G. K. Beale and D. A. Carson, eds., *Commentary on the New Testament Use of the Old Testament* (Grand Rapids: Baker Academic, 2007), 944–47.

The psalmist beautifully portrays our place in creation, acknowledging that we exist a little lower than God. This positioning just below God places us at the pinnacle of God's creative masterpiece. We stand above all other creatures as the apex of God's creation, crowned with dignity and majesty.

Furthermore, Psalm 8 echoes our calling to exercise dominion over creation (Gen. 1:26, 28). Likewise, Psalm 115:16 affirms that God has given the earth to the sons of men. This mandate finds fulfillment in passages like James 3, where the authority we possess over all created beings is shown to be accomplished. Mankind has fulfilled its creation mandate to such an extent that the apostle can say, "Every species of beasts and birds, of reptiles and creatures of the sea, is tamed and has been tamed by the human race" (v. 7). This dominion testifies to our distinction from the animal kingdom.

In addition, we cannot miss the astounding significance of the fact that we are "crown[ed] … with glory and majesty" by God Himself (Ps. 8:5). This bestowal of such dignity highlights both our privileged position of honor over all creation, as well as our responsibility as stewards to reflect God's glory in our rule over creation. As we have seen in the previous chapters, the preborn are fully human and truly children; therefore, they too share in this glory and honor.

Humans and animals are different

This section delves into the biblical foundations that affirm the inherent worth of human beings over animals, and explores how our physical,[39] intellectual, and spiritual attributes set us apart in the order of creation.

In a society increasingly advocating for animal rights and often equating animal and human life, it is vital to revisit the Scriptures to understand God's perspective. The Bible consistently emphasizes that while animals are part of God's creation and deserve humane treatment

---

39 See 1 Cor. 15:39.

to some extent, they do not share the same status as humans, who are uniquely designed to reflect God's image.

This understanding is crucial, especially in contemporary discussions where the value of human life, as seen in the issue of abortion, is frequently contested. By examining scriptural teachings, we can reaffirm the biblical worldview that upholds human dignity and worth above all other forms of life.

Different categories of creation

While some passages note similarities between humans and animals,[40] the Bible consistently distinguishes them as categorically distinct forms of creation. Humans are never called animals in Scripture.[41] Instead, there is always a clear line drawn between the two.

For example, throughout biblical history, divine judgments frequently affected both man and beast, yet they are always mentioned separately, proving their distinction in God's eyes. The plagues in Egypt afflicted both categories—whether through disease, hail, or death—demonstrating that while both were affected by God's actions, they remained separate entities in His dealings. "There were gnats on *man* and *beast*" (Exod. 8:17-18, emphasis mine). It was foretold that there would be "boils breaking out with sores on *man* and *beast*" (9:9-10, emphasis mine).[42] "He smote the firstborn of Egypt, both of *man* and *beast*" (Ps. 135:8, emphasis mine). Other passages describing national judgments similarly differentiate between man and beast by listing them sepa-

---

40   e.g., both man and animals receive life from God (Gen. 2:7; 7:22) and are dependent on His provision (Ps. 104:14, 27-29; Matt. 6:26). God preserves both (Ps. 36:6) and expresses concern for both in His dealings with creation (Jon. 4:11).

41   Some verses will say we behave *like* animals when we stoop down to their level of behavior (Pss. 49:20; 73:22; Titus 1:12; 2 Pet. 2:12; Jude 10). The closest possible reference to equating mankind and the animal kingdom would be Ecc. 3:18, but the following verses draw a clear distinction between man and beast as two distinct forms of creation.

42   For the distinction between man and beast in regards to the other plagues, see Exod. 9:19, 22, 25; 11:7; 12:12; 13:15.

rately.[43] However, God also speaks of restoring both, such as in Ezekiel 36:11, where He promises to "multiply ... man and beast" as a sign of blessing.

When God commanded that the firstborn be consecrated to Him, He made a clear distinction between human and animal life. This is evident not only in how He lists the two categories separately—requiring the firstborn of man *and* beast—but also in how He differentiates their treatment. The firstborn of both man and beast belonged to the Lord, yet the treatment of each differed: while animals could be sacrificed, human firstborns were to be redeemed (Exod. 13:2; Num. 3:13; 8:17; 18:15). This distinction reinforces the greater worth of human life in God's eyes.

David acknowledges that God "preserve[s] *man* and *beast*" (Ps. 36:6, emphasis mine). In Nineveh, God's mercy extended to both humans and animals. He distinguished these different forms of creation by stating, "Should I not have compassion on Nineveh, the great city in which there are more than 120,000 *persons* who do not know the difference between their right and left hand, *as well as many animals*" (Jon. 4:11, emphasis mine; cf. 3:8)?

Other passages throughout the Bible further emphasize this separation. When the Israelites described the devastation of the land, they did so by stating that it was a desolation or a waste "without man or beast," again affirming their distinction as different forms of creation (Jer. 32:43; 33:12; cf. v. 10). Similarly, God is said to have made man and beast (Jer. 27:5) and to "sow the house of Israel and the house of Judah with the *seed of man* and with the *seed of beast*" (Jer. 31:27, emphasis mine), treating each as its own category.[44]

---

43 cf. Jer. 21:6; 36:29; 50:3; 51:62; Ezek. 14:21; 25:13; 29:8, 11; Zeph. 1:3.
44 See a similar distinction drawn between mankind and animals in Gen. 1:29-30; 9:2, 5; Exod. 19:13; Num. 31:11, 26, 47; Zech. 8:10. See also Lawrence O. Richards, "Animals," in *Expository Dictionary of Bible Words* (Grand Rapids, MI: Zondervan, 1985), 51–53.

Our minds are different

The Bible consistently distinguishes mankind from animals regarding our mental capacities. One of the gifts stemming from being made in God's image is the sophistication of our minds, enabling us to fulfill our mandate to rule over creation. For example, Job 35:11 notes that God "teaches us more than the beasts of the earth and makes us wiser than the birds of the heavens."

Scripture consistently teaches this distinction in intelligence between creatures bearing God's image and those that do not. Bildad, in his complaint to Job, recognized this division: "Why are we regarded as beasts, as stupid in your eyes" (Job 18:3)? Psalm 32:9 says, "Do not be as the horse or as the mule which have no understanding." Psalm 49:20 says, "Man in his pomp, yet without understanding, is like the beasts that perish."[45] Asaph writes, "I was senseless and ignorant; I was like a beast before You" (Ps. 73:22). Hosea 7:11 says, "Ephraim has become like a silly dove, without sense." God describes for Job the rather odd behavior of an ostrich and concludes they are this way, "Because God has made her forget wisdom, and has not given her a share of under-standing" (Job 39:17).

Nebuchadnezzar lived like an animal

This contrast between humans and animals is vividly portrayed in the real life example of Nebuchadnezzar being humbled by the Lord (Dan. 4). Initially shown in a vision, it is decreed that he would undergo a transformation: "Let his mind be changed from that of a man and let a beast's mind be given to him" (v. 16).[46] How could God have more clearly distinguished between man and beast?

---

45 While the point of comparison in this verse is that both men and animals *perish*—not that both are *stupid*—the psalmist states that these men do not contemplate spiritual or eternal matters but only focus on the present. This is why their fate is the same as that of animals, which do the same.

46 It is important to note that the Hebrew word for "mind" in this verse is literally "heart," encompassing the spiritual aspect of our being rather than mere cognitive function.

Later in the chapter, the vision is fulfilled as the king is driven away to live among the animals until his human reason returns to him (vv. 28-37). The term used for his "reason" (vv. 34, 36) refers to *knowledge* or *understanding*, making a clear distinction between the intelligence of humans and other creatures.

When God removed the king's human ability to reason, he regressed into a state akin to a wild animal. Note how verse 32 explicitly separates mankind from beasts: "You will be driven away from mankind, and your dwelling place will be with the beasts of the field."

More valuable than sparrows

In the Gospels, Jesus emphasizes the intrinsic value of human beings by comparing and contrasting them with birds and farm animals. In Matthew 6:26, our Lord points out that God cares for the birds, providing for their needs, yet by comparison humans are "worth much more" than they are. This comparison highlights the special status of humanity in God's creation.

In Matthew 10:31, Jesus reiterates this by assuring His followers that they are "more valuable than many sparrows." This statement confirms God's deep concern and care for each individual. Similarly, in Matthew 12:12, He argues that humans are "much more valuable … than a sheep," reinforcing the idea that human life has great significance above the rest of creation.

Jesus uses lesser-to-greater logic in Luke 13:15-16 to show that a woman is far more valuable than an ox. He says:

> You hypocrites, does not each of you on the Sabbath untie his ox or his donkey from the stall and lead him away to water him? And this woman, a daughter of Abraham as she is, whom Satan has bound for eighteen long years, should she not have been released from this bond on the Sabbath day?

In Matthew 8:28-34, the apostle gives his eyewitness account of Jesus healing the Gadarene demoniac. Here, Jesus demonstrated the elevated value He placed on mankind over the animal kingdom. He exorcised demons from the man, granting their request to enter a herd of pigs, which then rushed into the water and drowned (v. 32). Despite the herd being large and containing "many swine" (v. 30), Jesus prioritized saving the possessed man over the pigs, demonstrating His greater compassion for mankind. Just one human being was more precious to Jesus than *many* swine.[47]

This same principle of mankind's superior value is reflected in the Mosaic Law, where the penalty for murdering a human far exceeds that for killing an animal. Leviticus 24:21 stipulates that for killing an animal, restoration suffices; however, for killing a human being, capital punishment is required (cf. vv. 17-18). Moreover, Old Testament laws concerning animal restitution were not for the animal's sake but for the benefit of the human owner, who received blessings from the animals' provision.

Human rights over animal rights

When my wife and I adopted our first rescue dog, he had burn marks where his previous owner had put out cigarettes on him. That's horrible! I hope reading that made you feel disgusted or angry. My point is that while the Bible emphasizes mankind's value over the animal kingdom, it does not advocate for mistreating animals. Scripture affirms that "a righteous man has regard for the life of his animal" (Prov. 12:10). The Law includes guidelines on the proper treatment of animals (e.g., Exod. 23:4-5; Deut. 22:1-4).[48] We are called to maintain the biblical perspective that mankind, made in God's image, is to rule *responsibly* over the animal kingdom—not as *tyrants*.

However, keeping perspective and maintaining a biblical balance is crucial. Certain animal rights cases—such as Cecil the Lion, Harambe the Gorilla, and Penka the Cow—captured international attention. I

---

47 It is noteworthy that Jesus never did the opposite—harming a human to save an animal.

48 Again, in these texts, the main concern is that the animal is an enemy's or neighbor's source of food and resources. The emphasis remains on benefiting humans who depend on the animal rather than on the animal itself.

Mankind Distinct from Animals

bring these up not to offer personal opinions on these cases but to highlight the world's disproportionate values. While there was an outcry over the death of a single animal in a distant land, the deaths of thousands of children in our own backyards barely raise an eyebrow.

Our outrage should be redirected to the gravest injustice in human history: legalized abortion. While supporting animal rights is certainly permissible, elevating their rights above human life distorts the moral order God established. This confusion is evident in modern ethical debates, where some people fiercely advocate for animal welfare yet support abortion—the deliberate taking of innocent human life. If we are to follow a biblical ethic, we must recognize that while animals should be treated with kindness, human life must always take precedence. We must prioritize our efforts and resources, giving due regard to human suffering.

This exploration of the biblical distinction between humans and animals reaffirms that humans are uniquely created in the image of God, imparting a higher value to human life than to animal life. This theological understanding explains why abortion is of grave concern: it involves the murder of one made in God's image—a crime far greater than squashing a mosquito!

As Christians, our worldview must be shaped by this biblical truth. While we are called to treat animals with kindness and respect, we must never lose sight of the greater responsibility of respecting and protecting human beings. The distinction God established at creation should guide our ethical and moral decisions, ensuring we prioritize protecting human life.

–4–

God Hates the Shedding of Innocent Blood

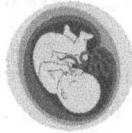

T he act of shedding innocent blood, as in the case of abortion, is not new. Although the blood of children was shed in different ways and for different reasons, this most grievous offense against God's moral order has a long, dark history. The Scriptures consistently depict the shedding of innocent blood as an abomination that provokes God's anger and incites His judgment.

The relevance of these biblical texts to the modern issue of abortion lies in their unwavering condemnation of acts that violate the sanctity of life. Abortion, viewed through this biblical lens, cannot be written off as merely a "social" or "political" issue where God's opinion of the matter has no authority. We must always remember that God's Word has authority over every area of our lives. As we examine the biblical passages that address the shedding of innocent blood, we find that God is deeply grieved by such acts and holds nations and individuals accountable for their complicity in these sins. This exploration aims to connect the dots, demonstrating that the Scriptural condemnations of such practices affirm the enduring truth that God condemns the practice of abortion in our day.

Innocent bloodshed is abominable

The repugnant act of shedding innocent blood is frequently and consistently condemned in Scripture. This abhorrent practice is consistently deemed "abominable" and "detestable" in the Bible. For example, God warned Israel not to imitate the abominable practices of the nations they were dispossessing, which included child sacrifice and other detestable acts tied to shedding innocent blood (Deut. 18:9–14). King Ahaz walked in those same wicked ways, even burning his own son as an offering, copying the nations God had cast out (2 Kgs. 16:3); and later, King Manasseh did even more evil by following pagan nations, building altars to idols, and shedding very much innocent blood throughout Jerusalem, provoking God's wrath (2 Kgs. 21:2–9).

God condemned the people through Jeremiah for building high places to Baal in the Valley of Hinnom, where they burned their sons and daughters in the fire—a thing He never commanded but considered a vile abomination (Jer. 32:35). Through Ezekiel, He reminded Jerusalem of her unfaithfulness and failure to remember her early days, multiplying her abominations with idol worship and bloodshed, including child sacrifice (Ezek. 16:22). Later, God declared that the people had defiled themselves with idols and murdered their children as sacrifices, prompting judgment for these detestable acts (Ezek. 23:36).

God explicitly declares that He *hates* the shedding of innocent blood (Deut. 12:31; Prov. 6:16-17). It evokes a visceral response from God, kindling His anger and provoking divine displeasure (2 Kgs. 17:17, 18; 21:6; Jer. 7:30). God finds it loathsome.[49]

Throughout the Scriptures, this horrendous act is a desecration that defiles and profanes (Lev. 20:3; Jer. 7:30-31; Ezek. 23:37-38). God spoke through Ezekiel: "I pronounced them *unclean* because of their gifts, in that they caused all their firstborn to pass through the fire" (Ezek. 20:26, emphasis mine). Later He says, "When you offer your

---

49 In the biblical narratives, shedding innocent blood is often "the breaking point when God moves from patiently warning to active judgment" (John Ensor, *Answering the Call: Saving Innocent Lives One Woman at a Time* [Peabody: Hendrickson, 2012], 57).

gifts, when you cause your sons to pass through the fire, you are *defiling* yourselves with your idols to this day" (v. 31, emphasis mine). This defilement extends beyond the individual perpetrators to the land itself, as seen in explicit references to bloodshed defiling the land.[50]

This detestable sin incites divine retribution. The severity of this transgression is evident in how it invokes divine judgment upon the perpetrators. God holds those who engage in such practices guilty (Deut. 19:10). God punishes them. For example, God threatened that He would set His face against a man who commits such an act, and will cut him off from the people, even ordering that he be put to death (Lev. 20:1-5). The Lord brought enemies against the people to destroy them for participating in these acts.[51]

The history of Israel's conquest of Canaan demonstrates God's anger toward innocent bloodshed, as He judged the nations inhabiting the land for their grievous sins, including child sacrifice and bloodshed. Their widespread violence led to their expulsion from the land. God warned His people, "When you enter the land which the LORD your God gives you, you shall not learn to imitate the *detestable* things of those nations. There shall not be found among you anyone who makes his son or his daughter pass through the fire … For whoever does these things is *detestable* to the LORD; and *because of these detestable things* the LORD your God will drive them out before you" (Deut. 18:9-12, emphasis mine). God calls passing children through fire "the abominations of the nations whom the LORD had driven out from before the sons of Israel" (2 Kgs. 16:3; cf. 21:2-9).

These passages about shedding innocent blood highlight its grievousness and show us how God feels about the shedding of innocent blood in our own day. God both *hates* and *abominates* abortion.

---

50 Gen. 4:10; Lev. 18:21, 25; Num. 35:33; Ps. 106:38; Ezek. 36:18; Hos. 6:8.
51 e.g., Under King Jehoiakim, the Lord sent raiding bands from Babylon, Aram, Moab, and Ammon as judgment, specifically because of the innocent blood he had shed, which the Lord was not willing to forgive (2 Kgs. 24:2–4; cf. 17:17-18; Ps. 106:40-43).

Examples of innocent bloodshed

Having examined a concise summary of the biblical testimony of God's abhorrence of shedding innocent blood, we now hone in on particular passages that mention this vicious act. Those texts that speak of sacrifices to Molech will be examined in the next chapter. For now, we look at killing the innocent more generally.

The Bible offers a compelling indictment against the shedding of innocent blood. This theme runs deep through the prophetic literature. These Scriptures, while addressing the specific historical context of Israel's infidelity and idolatry, establish the timeless truth of the sanctity of human life. These prophetic denunciations unequivocally reflect God's anger toward the shedding of innocent blood. This truth bears unavoidable implications for the contemporary issue of abortion.

Blood on your hands (Isa. 1)

Isaiah cries out, "When you spread out your hands in prayer, I will hide My eyes from you; Yes, even though you multiply prayers, I will not listen. *Your hands are covered with blood*" (Isa. 1:15, emphasis mine)! In this context, the people of God bring their offerings to God and yet He rejects them because they have shed blood. It may be tempting to interpret the "blood" here as referring only to the excessive animal sacrifices mentioned in verse 11. However, a closer examination reveals that this interpretation is insufficient for several reasons, and we should instead understand this as a reference to the shedding of innocent *human* blood.

Firstly, verse 21 of the same chapter explicitly mentions murders occurring in the city. The prophet Isaiah, therefore, is addressing not just religious hypocrisy but also the people's violent sins. The "blood" on their hands is not the blood of goats and bulls, but of human beings they have murdered, either literally or indirectly through neglect.

Secondly, the surrounding context emphasizes the mistreatment of the oppressed, the orphan, and the widow (v. 17). This concern for social justice shows that the "blood" on their hands is more likely human.

God Hates the Shedding of Innocent Blood

Thirdly, the idea that God is merely disapproving of sacrifices themselves misses the point. The issue is not with the act of sacrifice in and of itself but with the heart condition of those offering them. God abhors sacrifices offered by those who harbor unrepentant sin in their lives. The surrounding context shows that this unrepented sin involves harming innocent human lives.

Fourthly, the theme of blood-stained hands is a recurring biblical metaphor for guilt in murder (e.g., Ezek. 3:18-20; 33:8; Matt. 27:24). This means it is far more likely that human blood which they have violently shed is on their hands.

Finally, it is noteworthy that, in biblical Hebrew, the plural form of "blood" is never used to refer to the blood of animals.[52]

Were they actually killing the innocent?

In this passage, Isaiah unequivocally condemns the shedding of blood. Contextually, this most likely includes active violence perpetrated against another human being. This is evident for the following reasons.

First, the Hebrew word for "blood" in this verse is in the plural form, which intensifies its meaning. Rather than suggesting multiple *bloods*, the plural form can signify ideas of *much* blood, *large quantities* of blood, or *gushing* blood. Thus, Isaiah is not merely accusing them of negligence but of significant and widespread bloodshed.[53]

Secondly, verse 21 explicitly labels the people as "murderers." While this term does not necessarily imply that the inhabitants of Jerusalem

---

52 G. Johannes Botterweck and Helmer Ringgren, eds., *Theological Dictionary of the Old Testament*, vol. 3, trans. John T. Willis (Grand Rapids: Eerdmans, 1978), 236.

53 "Of abundance, blood in quantity, hence [sometimes] of blood shed by rude violence, and of blood-stains." Francis Brown, S. R. Driver, and Charles A. Briggs, *A Hebrew and English Lexicon of the Old Testament*, trans. Edward Robinson (Oxford: Clarendon, 1906), s.v. דָּם. Young points out that *damim* denotes "violently shed blood" in Edward J. Young, *The Book of Isaiah: The English Text, with Introduction, Exposition, and Notes*, vol. 1, *Chapters 1-18* (Grand Rapids: Eerdmans, 1965), 69. Motyer suggests "deeds of blood-guiltiness" in J. Alec Motyer, *The Prophecy of Isaiah: An Introduction and Commentary* (Downers Grove: InterVarsity, 1993), 47.

were engaging in direct acts of murder, such as going house to house shooting and stabbing people, it does indicate a level of culpability in causing death. Neglecting to care for the vulnerable, such as widows, orphans, and the poor, is in the prophet's eyes tantamount to murder.

This concept is echoed in James 5:1-6, where the withholding of wages is linked to the death of laborers, and in Jeremiah 22, which speaks of innocent blood being shed through dishonest gain, oppression, and extortion (see below). Psalm 94:6 further illustrates how the killing of the innocent often occurs through such injustice: "They slay the widow and the stranger and murder the orphans." In other words, a hands-off, indirect action that leads to starvation is still murder.

While Isaiah's primary focus is on the shedding of literal blood, the prophet's denunciation of neglect toward the widow and orphan (v. 17) demonstrates that God holds His people accountable for all actions—and inactions—that lead to the loss of innocent life. Whether through active violence or passive indifference, the result is the same: the shedding of innocent blood. God is deeply concerned for the protection of the most vulnerable in society. The shedding of innocent blood in any form is an abomination to Him.

God's wrath against the shedding of innocent blood encompasses both overt acts of violence, such as child sacrifice, and the neglect of society's most vulnerable. For the church today, this reinforces our call to oppose all forms of injustice, particularly abortion, which is the most direct and heinous form of innocent bloodshed in our time. Yet it also challenges us to actively protect and care for the vulnerable—through advocacy and practical support—at every stage of life.

Mistreatment of the vulnerable (Jer. 22)

Jeremiah 22 reveals that God abhors the oppression of the marginalized and the shedding of innocent blood (vv. 3, 13, 17). While the sins highlighted in this chapter may seem to stem more from neglect than outright violence, the condemnation of such injustices as oppression and violence is unmistakably clear.

God Hates the Shedding of Innocent Blood

Consider the prophet's focus on God's unyielding command for justice and righteousness, especially toward the marginalized. He calls us to protect the stranger, the fatherless, and the widow, emphasizing that true justice involves active care and defense of the vulnerable.

> Do justice and righteousness, and deliver the one who has been robbed from the power of his oppressor. Also do not mistreat or do violence to the stranger, the orphan, or the widow; and do not shed innocent blood in this place. (Jeremiah 22:3)

On the other hand, the oracle shows that God's response to the oppressors is severe. Verses 5 and following depict a threat of desolation upon those who perpetuate injustice, highlighting the recurring biblical theme of divine retribution against killing the innocent. This is not merely a casual warning but a declaration of certain judgment. God invokes His own name, making this a solemn oath that guarantees the fulfillment of His warnings of judgment against such violence.[54]

In addition, the pronouncement of "woe" in verse 13 intensifies the warning, signifying that severe calamity awaits those who exploit others for unjust gain. This strong language shows the seriousness of these offenses and God's firm stance against such wrongdoing.

Jeremiah 22, therefore, advocates for the protection of the oppressed. Whether the oppression is through neglect or direct violence, the message is clear: God hates the mistreatment of the vulnerable.

The literal sacrifice of children (Ps. 106)

Psalm 106 recounts Israel's abominable practice of child sacrifice, a sin they adopted by mingling with pagan nations.

> They even sacrificed their sons and their daughters to the demons,

---

54 cf. Isa. 62:8; Jer. 44:26; 49:13; Amos 4:2; 6:8; 8:7. In Isa. 45:23, for God to swear by Himself means what was spoken "will not turn back," meaning whatever is sworn in such a way, God will not reverse. Moreover, in Heb. 6:13-18, the author explains how God swearing by Himself to Abraham (Gen. 22:16) assures that what was spoken is unchangeable. So here in Jeremiah, God will surely bring this punishment to pass.

> And shed innocent blood,
> The blood of their sons and their daughters,
> Whom they sacrificed to the idols of Canaan;
> And the land was polluted with the blood. (Psalm 106:37-38)

This heinous act provoked the Lord's displeasure, leading to their destruction by other nations. The text provides compelling evidence that this was indeed child sacrifice.

First, the passage describes the land as being "polluted with ... blood," a phrase that means murder and desecration have taken place there.[55] This recurring biblical phrase emphasizes the seriousness of their sin, as evidenced by the grave consequences of such actions.

Second, the use of the word "sacrificed" twice in this passage clearly indicates the deliberate killing of children, a direct violation of God's commandments and a reflection of the idolatrous influence of surrounding nations. This explicit terminology leaves no doubt about the nature of Israel's sin.

Third, the term "shed[ding] ... blood" frequently refers to killing.[56] For example, Deuteronomy 19:10 uses the term in reference to cities of refuge for murderers, and Deuteronomy 21:7 uses it concerning a slain human body. Moreover, the term is often used for pouring the blood of sacrificed animals onto the ground.[57]

The only potential exception from this standard meaning of murder or sacrifice occurs in 1 Kings 18:28, where the Baal worshipers cut themselves. However, even in that context, the act is seen as violent and displeasing to God. Thus, even if Psalm 106:37-38 were interpreted in that way, it still denotes a horrific and abominable practice.

In conclusion, Psalm 106:37-38 contains a clear condemnation of Israel's grievous sin: the literal shedding of innocent blood through the abhorrent practice of child sacrifice. This is a sobering reminder of God's unwavering stance against the shedding of innocent blood,

---

55 Gen. 4:10; Lev. 18:25; Num. 35:33; Ezek. 36:18; Hos. 6:8.
56 Gen. 9:6; 2 Kgs. 24:4; Isa. 59:7; Ezek. 22:1-5; Zeph. 1:17.
57 Exod. 29:12; Lev. 4:7, 18, 25, 30, 34; 17:13; Deut. 12:16, 24, 27; 15:23; Ezek. 24:7.

which is relevant in contemporary discussions about the sanctity of life and the moral implications of abortion.

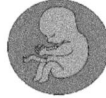

The biblical witness against shedding innocent blood provides a clear and compelling theological foundation for understanding God's stance on the sanctity of life. The repeated condemnation of such practices teaches that life, especially that of the most vulnerable, is inviolable.

This truth directly confronts the modern practice of abortion, which, like the ancient practices of the disobedient Israelites, represents a disregard for the sanctity of life. God's people must stand against such violent sins, advocating for the protection of all innocent lives. As we reflect on these passages, may we be moved to uphold and proclaim the value of life, aligning our hearts with God's compassionate concern for the defenseless and the innocent in our midst.

–5–

Passing Through Fire
to Molech

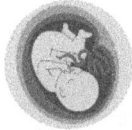

I n the previous chapter, we explored biblical passages that con-
demn the murder of the innocent in general. This chapter deals
specifically with the horrific ritual of passing children through
fire to false god Molech. The Bible, particularly through prohibition in
the Mosaic Law and through prophetic preaching, portrays God's consistent condemnation of such practices.

This chapter seeks to explore the depths of God's holy displeasure
against child sacrifice. Examining the historical and theological contexts
informs our understanding of the gravity of these sins. By doing so, it
aims to draw a direct parallel to the contemporary issue of abortion,
highlighting the timeless nature of God's view on the sanctity of life.

Whether or not one goes so far as to draw an exact, one-for-one
parallel to the modern practice of abortion, stating that the mother sacrifices her unborn child to the god of money, beauty, or self, the
connection is still valid, and these texts are still relevant to the issue of
abortion. The baby does not need to be "sacrificed" to an "idol" in order to constitute a violation of these commands.

Indeed, these passages do not explicitly mention abortion. However, the connection is not far-fetched. The biblical denunciation of
child sacrifice—where innocent children were cruelly sacrificed to idols
—closely parallels abortion, where unborn lives are ended in the womb.
Both practices, although different in form and cultural context, involve
killing the innocent.

"Pass through" (no mention of fire)

Often the idolatrous practice was described as passing the child
"through fire," specifically. But other times the same ritual was described without an explicit mention of fire. We will explore these latter
contexts first before examining the more explicit verses afterward.

Leviticus 20:2-5 unequivocally declares God's stance against these
abominable acts, prescribing the death penalty for the perpetrators:

> Any man from the sons of Israel or from the aliens sojourning in
> Israel who gives any of his offspring to Molech,[58] shall surely be put
> to death; the people of the land shall stone him with stones. I will
> also set My face against that man and will cut him off from among
> his people, because he has given some of his offspring to Molech,
> so as to defile My sanctuary and to profane My holy name. If the
> people of the land, however, should ever disregard that man when
> he gives any of his offspring to Molech, so as not to put him to
> death, then I Myself will set My face against that man and against
> his family, and I will cut off from among their people both him and
> all those who play the harlot after him, by playing the harlot after
> Molech.

---

58 Rather than referring to the name of the false god Molech, here—as well
as in Lev. 18:21; 2 Kgs. 23:10; Jer. 32:35—the Hebrew term may refer instead to a specific type of sacrifice or offering. See J. Gray, "Molech,
Moloch," in George Arthur Buttrick, ed., *The Interpreter's Dictionary of the
Bible: An Illustrated Encyclopedia*, vol. 3, *K-Q* (Nashville: Abingdon, 1962),
422–23; J. A. Thompson, "Molech, Moloch," in J. D. Douglas, ed., *New
Bible Dictionary* 2nd ed. (Leicester: Inter-Varsity, 1982), 789–90. Whether offered to this particular idol or more generally, human sacrifice
undoubtedly still occurred.

Likewise, Ezekiel 20:25-32 shows the severity of this transgression. This passage highlights God's judgment on Israel for participating in such detestable practices, revealing the spiritual corruption that had infiltrated their worship. God expresses how in doing so, the Israelites had "blasphemed" Him, and acted "treacherously" against Him (v. 27). It was a "detestable" act that "defile[d]" them (vv. 30-31).

In Jeremiah 32:35, God expresses His utter abhorrence for the practice, noting that such a thing had never even crossed His mind (cf. 7:31; 19:5)! Such unimaginable horror is associated with these practices.

This strong biblical denunciation of child sacrifice serves as a forceful reminder of God's unwavering commitment to protect innocent life. The act of sacrificing children to Molech is portrayed as not only a crime against the children themselves but also as an affront to God. Today, this ancient condemnation resonates with the church's stance against abortion, which is a modern-day parallel to child sacrifice.

Food for the gods

Another way the biblical prophets vividly depict this awful act is by describing the sacrifice as food for the gods. For example, Ezekiel says:

> Son of man, will you judge Oholah and Oholibah? Then declare to them their abominations. For they have committed adultery, and blood is on their hands. Thus they have committed adultery with their idols and even caused their sons, whom they bore to Me, to pass through the fire to them as food. Again, they have done this to Me; they have defiled My sanctuary on the same day and have profaned My sabbaths. For when they had slaughtered their children for their idols, they entered My sanctuary on the same day to profane it; and lo, thus they did within My house. (Ezekiel 23:36-39)

Although the term "fire" is absent from the original Hebrew, and verse 37 only mentions "pass[ing] through" to the gods, the context nonetheless suggests the grim reality that these children were burned or even offered as "food" for pagan deities.

In other prophetic texts from Ezekiel, the term "food" alludes to consumption by fire (Ezek. 15:4, 6; 21:32),[59] indicating the gruesome fate of these innocent lives. Furthermore, the word "slaughtered" in this passage (23:39), frequently associated with sacrificial rituals, intensifies the abhorrence of this practice.

Ezekiel 16:20-21 also speaks of children being slaughtered and passed through to the gods:

> Moreover, you took your sons and daughters whom you had borne to Me and sacrificed them to idols to be devoured. Were your harlotries so small a matter? You slaughtered My children and offered them up to idols by causing them to pass through the fire.

The rhetoric employed by Ezekiel, such as the litotes in verse 20 —"Were your harlotries so small a matter?"—serves as a powerful device that emphasizes the enormity of the transgression. This figure of speech highlights the shock and outrage these acts provoked in God. Rather than being trivial, they are matters of immeasurable importance to God.

This practice of offering children to Molech, far from being a mere ritualistic devotion, encapsulates a repugnant and profane offense against God, eliciting His severe displeasure. Even when "fire" is not mentioned, contextual clues often indicate that burning took place.

These denunciations from long ago are a call to protect the most vulnerable against any similar atrocities that persist in our world.

Where "fire" is explicitly mentioned

The biblical references that explicitly mention the act of children passing through fire unveil a deeper, more disturbing facet of the practice associated with Molech worship. These passages include undeniable references to the literal burning of children as a sacrifice.

Deuteronomy 12:31 unequivocally condemns this practice as abominable and detestable to God, stating, "You shall not behave thus

---

59 אָכְלָה. In these texts, the KJV translates the word as "fuel" for the fire.

Passing Through Fire to Molech

toward the LORD your God, for every abominable act which the LORD hates they have done for their gods; for they even burn their sons and daughters in the fire to their gods." The clear reference to fire in this context of child sacrifice demonstrates the gravity of this transgression, reflecting a consistent biblical stance against such horrendous acts (cf. 18:10).

The historical account in 2 Kings 23:10 vividly portrays King Josiah's commendable eradication of these sacrificial practices. "He also defiled Topheth, which is in the valley of the son of Hinnom, that no man might make his son or his daughter pass through the fire for Molech." The mention of "fire" substantiates the association between Molech worship and the terrifying act of passing children through literal flames (cf. 1 Kgs. 11:7).

The prophet Ezekiel highlights the defilement caused by such actions, emphasizing the spiritual consequences of this abominable practice and its hindrance to prayer and worship.

"When you offer your gifts, when you cause your sons to pass through the fire, you are defiling yourselves with all your idols to this day. And shall I be inquired of by you, O house of Israel? As I live," declares the Lord GOD, "I will not be inquired of by you." (Ezekiel 20:31; cf. v. 3)

Also, from the parallel between verse 31, which mentions "pass[ing] through *fire*," and verse 26, which simply mentions "pass[ing] through," we see that, to the prophet, fire does not need to be mentioned in order for the phrase to refer to the most abominable practice. This sheds light on the verses mentioned in the previous section.

The biblical account in 2 Kings 16:3 (// 2 Chr. 28:3) reveals the grievousness of King Ahaz's actions in making his sons pass through fire. "But he walked in the way of the kings of Israel, and even made his son pass through the fire, according to the abominations of the nations whom the LORD had driven out from before the sons of Israel." This act, condemned as an abomination, is linked to the Lord's wrath upon other nations.

In 2 Kings 17:17, Israel's captivity in Assyria is attributed in part to this grave transgression. "Then they made their sons and their daughters pass through the fire, and practiced divination and enchantments, and sold themselves to do evil in the sight of the LORD, provoking Him." The fact that God was "very angry" (v. 18) signifies an intense anger ignited by Israel's heinous form of idolatry. The punishment is not just physical exile but also spiritual estrangement from God.

Jeremiah sheds light on the gravity of this practice, employing language laden with moral repugnance:

> "For the sons of Judah have done that which is evil in My sight," declares the LORD, "they have set their detestable things in the house which is called by My name, to defile it. They have built the high palaces of Topheth, which is in the valley of the son of Hinnom, to burn their sons and their daughters in the fire, which I did not command, and it did not come into My mind." (Jeremiah 7:30-31)

The words "defile," "evil," and "detestable" signify how heinous these actions were and how they incurred God's vehement displeasure. Jeremiah's strong language shows the repulsion these acts elicited from God. The people's frightening punishment is specified in verses 32-34.

"Burning" means burning!

The discussion surrounding the terms *burning* or *fire* in these passages demands further examination. Some interpreters attempt to whitewash the practice as something less than the literal burning of children alive in sacrifice to an idol.[60] Others may draw a parallel between passing through to Molech and the consecration of firstborns in Exodus 13:12. We might conclude that God's disappointment rests solely in the fact that they are dedicating the child to a god other than Himself. However, historical, linguistic, and exegetical evidence makes it clear that this ancient practice was as heinous as it sounds.

---

60 For example, see Keil and Delitzsch's commentary on Lev. 18:21.

The term itself denotes a destructive burning distinct from ordinary fire or metaphorical usage.[61] This was not a mere purification ritual or a symbolic act of consecration. Rather, the devastating reality is that it involved the complete consumption of the child by fire.

For example, the term's use in 2 Kings 17:31, describing sacrifices to the gods Adrammelech and Anammelech, speaks of burning their children in fire.

Jeremiah 19:4-5 confirms this understanding, using the same term to describe the burning of sons as a burnt offering to Baal. The concept of a burnt offering in biblical terms inherently implies total consumption by fire. This terminology clearly signifies the full sacrifice of the child, not a mere symbolic act.

These passages collectively serve as a moral indictment against the practice of child sacrifice. The repeated and explicit condemnation of these practices in Scripture show us God's displeasure of abortion, a practice with many similarities, even though it is not necessarily a sacrifice to a pagan idol.

God's wrath against burning of children

In 2 Kings 21:6 (// 2 Chr. 33:6), we encounter a deeply troubling depiction of practices described as very evil:

> He [Manasseh] made his son pass through the fire, practiced witchcraft and used divination, and dealt with mediums and spiritists. He did much evil in the sight of the LORD provoking Him to anger.

The passage speaks later on of Manasseh's reign which was marked by the wicked act of shedding "very much innocent blood" (v. 16).

The text's use of the term "provoking" the Lord highlights the intensity of divine indignation and anger elicited by these acts. This term is frequently used in contexts where God's wrath is incited by Israel's

---

61   See R. Laird Harris, Gleason L. Archer Jr., and Bruce K. Waltke, eds., *Theological Wordbook of the Old Testament* (Chicago: Moody, 1980), s.v. שָׂרַף.

sins.[62] This shows the severity of these actions, which aroused God's righteous anger and displeasure.

Most importantly, Judah's exile is explicitly attributed to Manasseh's sin (2 Kgs. 24:2-4; Jer. 15:1-4). This highlights the devastating conse-quences of such egregious sins. Manasseh's reign serves as a stark reminder of the severity of actions that provoke divine retribution, ulti-mately leading to Judah's exile. It vividly demonstrates the importance of upholding the sanctity of life, and reinforces the call for national leaders to walk in obedience to Christ's commands.

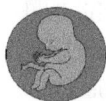

Scripture reveals the full extent of God's abhorrence toward the sin of child sacrifice, especially as it involved the burning of innocent chil-dren. The consistent biblical testimony—detailing these acts as abominations that provoke divine wrath—leaves no doubt about the severity of these sins and the severe judgment they incur.

These historical practices are not merely confined to the ancient world but also bear strong parallels to abortion in our day. Therefore, these passages serve as a call for our nation to repent of the innocent blood it has shed and continues to shed to this very day.

---

62 *Ibid.*, s.v. מֹלֶךְ.

-6-

Rescue Those Being
Led to Slaughter

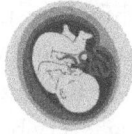

T he Christian is called to stand resolutely in defense of the defenseless. The Scriptures are replete with commands to protect the vulnerable, to act justly, and to show mercy. This mandate extends to the most innocent and helpless among us—the preborn children who are threatened with the violence of abortion.

Throughout the Old and New Testaments, God's heart for the oppressed and the downtrodden is made abundantly clear. The unborn child—who has no voice, no defender—is the epitome of the afflicted and needy whom we are called to protect.

The prophets of old consistently proclaimed the necessity of defending the orphan and pleading for the widow, which is not a far cry from defending the preborn child and the abandoned mother pressured into aborting them.

Rescue them from slaughter

God's command in Proverbs 24 is explicit and urgent: we are commanded to deliver those on the path to death, to intervene and hold back those staggering toward slaughter. This passage emphatically declarcs that ignorance is no excuse for inaction. Negligence is not merely passive; it is an active failure to uphold justice and compassion.

> Deliver those who are being taken away to death,
> And those who are staggering to slaughter, Oh hold them back.
> If you say, "See, we did not know this,"
> Does He not consider it who weighs the hearts?
> And does He not know it who keeps your soul?
> And will He not render to man according to his work? (Proverbs 24:11-12)

Despite its lack of popularity and even condemnation by many in the pro-life movement, preaching outside clinics finds clear justification in this passage.[63] In doing so, faithful Christians literally go right to where the violence takes place and call upon the mothers and doctors to repent and reconsider before it is too late. But if that heroic work is neither your gift nor your calling, every believer must still do something to protect the children.

This text is a call to courageous action—to step into the breach and offer rescue. To claim ignorance—"See, we did not know this"—is a grave misstep. God, who weighs our hearts and knows our souls,[64] sees through such excuses and will hold us accountable for our actions, or lack thereof. We cannot feign ignorance or remain passive; our faith demands active engagement in the battle to protect life.

Come to their rescue

Psalm 82 commands us to "vindicate," "do justice," "rescue," and "deliver" those in danger. These actions are not merely optional; they are

---

63   For biblical justification of the practice, see Randy C. Alcorn, *Is Rescuing Right?: Breaking the Law to Save the Unborn* (Downers Grove: InterVarsity, 1990), especially 182–99; Mark Belz, *Suffer the Little Children: Christians, Abortion, and Civil Disobedience* (Westchester: Crossway, 1989). While these sources may have been referring to more drastic measures of civil disobedience, their biblical justification applies to preaching outside of clinics.
64   1 Sam. 16:7; 1 Chr. 28:9; 2 Chr. 6:30; Pss. 7:9; 44:21; Jer. 11:20; 17:10.

imperatives rooted in the very character of God and His compassion for the oppressed.

> Vindicate the weak and fatherless;
> Do justice to the afflicted and destitute.
> Rescue the weak and needy;
> Deliver them out of the hand of the wicked. (Psalm 82:3-4)

To "vindicate" in this context means to intervene in a civil or domestic dispute, to adjudicate, or to enforce a just decision.[65] This term often denotes God's own vindication of those who have been wronged, as seen in Psalm 72:4, where He "vindicate[s] the afflicted of the people." The act of vindication involves stepping into situations of conflict and oppression, bringing the righteousness of God's judgment to bear and securing justice and safety for the afflicted.

The phrase "do justice" often refers to God delivering the needy. This term speaks to how God God defends the righteous and leads them in justice (Ps. 5:8), or how He tests hearts and brings justice to the oppressed (Jer. 11:20).[66] Isaiah states, "Zion shall be redeemed with justice, and her repentant ones with righteousness" (1:27).[67] God's justice is not passive but active, rectifying wrongs and establishing equality.

To "rescue" means to help someone escape from danger or to deliver them to safety. This particular term is used throughout the Psalms to describe God's interventions.[68] For example, Psalm 18:3 proclaims,

---

65 The Hebrew concept of vindication includes ruling justly in civil disputes (Prov. 29:14), defending orphans and advocating for the vulnerable in society (Isa. 1:17), judging with equity for the poor (Isa. 11:4), and calling out those who ignore justice and exploit the needy (Jer. 5:28). Christians are called to do this for unborn babies.

66 cf. Pss. 31:1; 37:6; 85:9-11; 97:2.

67 God appoints His Servant to be a light and bring justice to nations (Isa. 42:6), raises up deliverers in righteousness (Isa. 45:13), brings salvation and justice near (Isa. 46:13), stands up to vindicate His servant (Isa. 50:8), and calls His people to pursue justice and righteousness (Isa. 51:1).

68 God defeats violent enemies and delivers from the wicked (Pss. 17:13; 18:44, 49), saves those who trust in Him (22:5; 31:2), protects and rescues in times of trouble (37:40; 40:18), pleads the cause of the oppressed

"I call upon the LORD, who is worthy to be praised, and I am *saved* from my enemies" (emphasis mine). Our call to rescue the weak mirrors God's actions, demanding that we actively seek to save those in peril, reflecting His compassion.

Finally, we are to "deliver" those in distress. This word carries the connotation of snatching away from danger, a dramatic and decisive act of rescue. For instance, 1 Samuel 17:35 recounts David rescuing a lamb from the mouth of a lion (cf. Ezek. 34:10), and Joshua 2:13 speaks of Rahab's plea for deliverance from death.[69] The term is often used to describe how the Lord saved Israel from Egypt.[70] Deliverance is a recurring theme throughout Scripture, highlighting God's intervention in times of dire need (Ps. 7:1) or even spiritual deliverance.[71]

The commands in Psalm 82:3-4 are clear and compelling. We are to actively engage in vindicating, doing justice, rescuing, and delivering those who are oppressed and in danger. It is not hard to see how protecting the preborn from the imminent danger of abortion falls under these commands. We are to intervene on their behalf just as God intervenes on our behalf.[72]

Don't plug your ears—open your mouth!

Proverbs 21:13 warns, "He who shuts his ear to the cry of the poor will also cry himself and not be answered." Those who cover their eyes, turn their heads, walk past coldly, stop their ears, or pretend the suffering is not real are displeasing God by their inaction. This has serious

---

(43:1), comes quickly to help (70:6), brings deliverance in righteousness (71:2), rescues those who love Him (91:14), and is a stronghold and deliverer in battle (144:2).

69 cf. Pss. 33:19; 56:14; 86:14; Prov. 10:12; 11:4, 6; 23:14.

70 cf. Judg. 10:15; 1 Sam. 12:10; 1 Chr. 16:35.

71 cf. Pss. 39:8; 51:14; 69:14; 79:9.

72 Ensor points to Gen. 37:21-22; Exod. 1:17; 1 Sam. 14:45; 1 Kgs. 18:4; Esth. 4:14; 7:3-4 as examples from the rich history of God's people defending innocent life (*Answering the Call*, 83).

implications for Christians who are passive in the fight against abortion, or who deny the seriousness of the issue (cf. Prov. 28:27).

The "cry" here signifies an outcry of distress in the face of danger and desperation. This word is used in various contexts throughout Scripture to describe the lament of Mordecai (Esther 4:1), the righteous indignation of Nehemiah (Neh. 5:6), wailing amidst destruction (Jer. 51:54), heartbreak over ruin (Isa. 15:5), and terror in the face of invasion by raiders (Jer. 18:22). These cries are the sounds of human suffering that reach up to heaven, and God wants His people to respond. It has been an established scientific fact for a while now that the preborn feel pain and respond to touch.[73] Surely, they do cry out, but nobody hears except God alone.

Similarly, Proverbs 31:8-9 commands,

Open your mouth for the mute,
For the rights of all the unfortunate.
Open your mouth, judge righteously,
And defend the rights of the afflicted and needy.

This is a call to believers to be a voice for the voiceless. The unborn child, who cannot be heard and cannot stand up for themselves, requires our advocacy. The phrase "defend the rights" (KJV, "plead the cause") signifies rendering a judgment or making a ruling. This concept is deeply embedded in biblical justice and is often associated with God's intervention on behalf of His people.[74] Following God's example, we are to intervene on behalf of the preborn and plead their cause.

Furthermore, this advocacy is not merely a passive endorsement but an active engagement in their rescue from peril. In Psalm 35:1, David, using similar terminology, beseeches God: "*Contend*, O LORD, with those who contend with me; *fight* against those who fight against me"

---

73   See Jim Harrison, *Pro-Life: Saving the Lives of Unborn Children, Making Possible Their Descendants, and Helping Their Parents* (Maitland: Xulon Press, 2017), 35–38; Randy Alcorn, *Prolife Answers to Prochoice Objections*, 189–92.
74   cf. Pss. 9:4; 140:12; Jer. 5:28.

(emphasis mine).[75] In Psalm 43, the psalmist cries out, "*Vindicate* me, O God, and *plead my cause* against an ungodly nation" (v. 1, emphasis mine; cf. 119:154).

In light of this, our call to open our mouths for the unborn child who cannot be heard and to defend them from physical harm is a reflection of God's own justice and mercy. It is a call to action, urging us to stand in the gap for those who cannot defend themselves, being the voice for the voiceless. Jeremiah states that "plead[ing] the cause of the afflicted" is integral to knowing God (22:16; cf. Jas. 1:27-28).

Defend them and plead their cause

In Isaiah 1:17, God commands: "Learn to do good; seek justice, reprove the ruthless, defend the orphan, plead for the widow." This exhortation, while directed at corrupt leaders who exploit the vulnerable, is a general call to everyone to engage actively in the work of justice and compassion.

To "seek justice" is to pursue fairness and equity in all circumstances, ensuring that the scales are balanced for all people, particularly the downtrodden. This involves "reprov[ing] the ruthless," which means actively intervening and setting things right for those who are unjustly treated. This is not a passive stance but an active engagement in the struggle for justice.

The commands to "defend the orphan" and "plead for the widow" encompass both personal advocacy and legal intervention. To "plead" in this context means to dispute or quarrel on behalf of someone, often with legal connotations. This term frequently appears in Scripture with the nuance of conducting a legal suit or standing in court on behalf of the oppressed.[76]

This biblical perspective compels us to seek justice and mercy in tangible, everyday situations. We must mirror God's heart for the op-

---

75 cf. Isa. 49:25; Lam. 3:58; Mic. 7:9.
76 For example, God pleads the cause of the afflicted like a defense attorney in court (Prov. 22:23; Isa. 51:22). People cry out for God to take up their legal case against unjust accusers (Pss. 43:1; 119:154; Lam. 3:58).

pressed by standing in the gap for those who cannot defend themselves. We are called to not just feel pity, but to *actively* plead the cause of the marginalized.

Do justice and righteousness

The call to defend the needy is stated most clearly in Jeremiah 22. Here, God commands:

> Do justice and righteousness, and deliver the one who has been robbed from the power of his oppressor. Also do not mistreat or do violence to the stranger, the orphan, or the widow; and do not shed innocent blood in this place. (Jeremiah 22:3)

The term "robbed," or *spoiled,* signifies a forceful seizure, a violent taking away of property, often involving fraud, extortion, or ambush.[77] This term conveys not merely theft but a violent, oppressive act.

An "oppressor" is one who tramples the poor underfoot, exploiting their vulnerability. Throughout Scripture, God is portrayed as the Deliverer of the oppressed.[78] Oppression manifests in various forms, including withholding wages (Deut. 24:14; Jer. 22:13), accepting bribes to harm others (Ezek. 22:12), and committing acts of robbery and extortion (Lev. 6:2-4; Ezek. 22:29).[79]

The command in this verse to deliver from the power of an oppressor is a call to liberate those under the yoke of slavery or other unjust forces. This command addresses real-world injustices that affect the daily lives of the afflicted.

---

77 For example, God condemns those who defraud their neighbor or violently seize goods, linking robbery with covenant violation (Lev. 19:13; Ezek. 22:29). Such acts will bring judgment (Isa. 10:2; Prov. 22:22).
78 1 Chr. 16:21; Pss. 103:6; 105:14; 146:7.
79 The Hebrew word is also used in the context deceitful commerce (Hos. 12:7), exploiting positions of power for personal gain (1 Sam. 12:3-4), crushing the needy (Ps. 72:4; Amos 4:1), and perverting justice (Jer. 7:6; Zech. 7:10; Mal. 3:5).

This passage emphasizes the active role we must play in alleviating the suffering of the oppressed: we are to do justice and righteousness, intervening on behalf of those wronged.

The injunction not to mistreat the stranger, orphan, or widow emphasizes God's special concern for society's most vulnerable members. These individuals are often without defenders, making them easy targets for exploitation. The biblical call is to be their advocates, to ensure that their rights are upheld and that they are treated with dignity and respect.

Moreover, the command to "not shed innocent blood" serves as a stark reminder of the sanctity of life. It is a divine prohibition against acts of violence that harm or kill the innocent.

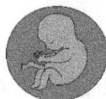

As we draw this chapter to a close, let us consider the gravity and urgency of our biblical mandate. The call to rescue those being led to slaughter is clear and unequivocal. As Christians, we are entrusted with the duty to defend the preborn—the most vulnerable among us—who face the terror of abortion in silence, behind closed doors.

Throughout this chapter, we have seen how the Bible consistently calls us to stand in the gap for the oppressed, to be a voice for the voiceless.

As we reflect on these Scriptures, we must recognize that silence and inaction in the face of abortion are not options. We cannot claim ignorance or hide behind excuses. The preborn, created in the image of God, are deserving of our protection and advocacy.

Let us commit ourselves to this calling with renewed vigor and determination. Let us rise to the challenge, empowered by the Holy Spirit, to be bold defenders of the innocent, to rescue those being led to slaughter, and to uphold the sanctity and dignity of every human life. In the next chapter we are going to explain how you and your church can help rescue unborn babies from abortion.

-7-

A Child-Friendly and Mother-Supportive Church

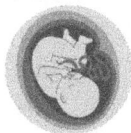

One of the greatest areas of impact we can have as Christians is how the gospel calls us to value children and to come alongside mothers within the church. In a society that often treats children as burdens and elevates personal convenience over the sanctity of life, the church must stand as a counter-cultural city on a hill.

In this chapter, we will explore steps toward creating a child-friendly and mother-supportive church. We begin with the heart of the matter: the gospel itself.

The gospel is preventive maintenance

The gospel changes everything, transforming hearts and minds to align with God's design for family, sexuality, and generosity. As the gospel takes root in our lives, it calls us to purity (Titus 2:11-14), urging believers to abstain from premarital sex (1 Thes. 4:3-8) and to uphold the sanctity of marriage (Heb. 13:4). While that alone would prevent most unplanned pregnancies, the transformation doesn't stop there! God's Word also renews our thinking about procreation, guiding us to see children not as inconveniences but as precious gifts from God to be cherished and nurtured (Ps. 127). The gospel molds hearts and lives, steering individuals away from sexual immorality and toward a life of purity and marital faithfulness. The transforming power of the gospel, as the Holy Spirit applies the preached Word to our hearts, acts as preventive maintenance for abortion, as believers' hearts are made obedient to Christ in all areas of life.

Abortions are often (though not always) chosen out of selfishness —such as fearing that having a baby will ruin one's career—or are driven by the lustful desire for sex without consequences. Only the gospel can enable a woman to overcome these passions through the victory that is in Christ. The Holy Spirit empowers believers to overcome these impulses and walk in obedience. By renewing our minds and aligning our desires with God's will, the gospel equips us to resist the temptations of the flesh and live in a manner that honors the Lord.

Furthermore, biblical preaching and teaching cultivate a culture of generosity within the church. As Christ's compassion toward helpless sinners is faithfully proclaimed, it softens hearts, encouraging believers to support the less fortunate and provide practical help to mothers in need. This generosity, fueled by and modeled after God's grace toward us in the gospel, offers struggling mothers support and alleviates her anxieties, transforming her doubts into courage and trust in God's provision. As these changes take root in the members' lives, the church can reflect Christ's own heart for preborn children and their mothers.

As more souls are saved and more biblical churches are planted, we cultivate a church culture infused with the sacrificial love of Christ. This gospel-centered transformation not only addresses issues that might lead a woman to consider abortion—such as poverty and broken families—but also strikes at the root causes by instilling godly virtues.

As the Word of God is faithfully preached and received, it prompts diligent labor to uphold the sanctity of life and inspires a spirit of open-handed generosity within the church.

While the gospel transforms individuals, the church as a whole can create structures of support for women and children. Within our congregations, ministries for children may flourish, nurturing the young while supporting families. The church becomes a refuge for those facing the challenges of unplanned pregnancies and financial hardship. A congregation of transformed hearts, gathered under one roof for worship, will create an environment where struggling mothers find support and children, if necessary, find homes through adoption. Older, more mature Christian women will mentor and guide younger women toward greater godliness, as outlined in Titus 2:3-5.

Each church must prayerfully consider how to apply these principles in its own setting, ministering to the specific needs of the specific women God brings their way. There is no single correct method that every church must follow. As we have seen, proclaiming the gospel and teaching Christian practice will lead God's people to do what is right.

The comfort God's Word brings

The solution to a woman's fears about providing for her child lies in the faithful preaching of life-giving truths of Scripture. The unchanging promise that God in Christ will never leave nor forsake her will turn her anxiety into steadfast courage (Deut. 31:6; Josh. 1:5; Heb. 13:5). Jesus' teachings on anxiety remind her of God's providential care, urging her to seek God's kingdom first (Matt. 6:25-34). God's paternal care, as illustrated in Matthew 7:7-11, reassures her of His loving provision. The secret of Christian contentment (Phil. 4:11) and the great gain in godliness with contentment (1 Tim. 6:6-8) will fill her heart, helping her to live comfortably with life's basic needs.

Likewise, biblical exhortations about possessions and generosity shape a church culture that supports women facing unplanned pregnancies. Through faithful preaching and discipleship, a community of believers emerges that is characterized by generosity and hospitality,[80] eager to share resources and meet each other's needs.[81] We follow the example of Christ, who emptied Himself to serve others (Phil. 2:4-11),

---

80 Rom. 12:13; Heb. 13:2; 1 Pet. 4:9.
81 Acts 2:44-45; 4:32-35; Gal. 6:10; Heb. 6:10.

who washed His disciples' feet (John 13), and who, though rich, became poor for our sake (2 Cor. 8:9). In a church filled with those ready to imitate His sacrificial love, no woman would feel pressured to choose abortion.

Reform your thoughts on procreation

Another crucial way the church can combat the culture of death is by reforming our own perspective on procreation and aligning our opinions with biblical principles. Many Christian couples today have adopted the world's view, seeing children as optional, a hindrance to personal ambitions, or even a burden. Yet the Scriptures paint a very different picture by presenting children as a blessing and an integral part of God's design for families and society (Ps. 127). We must resist the urge to call what God calls good "evil" (Isa. 5:20).[82]

This goes beyond debating whether or not the mandate to "be fruitful and multiply, and fill the earth" (Gen. 1:28; cf. 9:7) was limited to the ancient world. Rather, the entire Bible, from start to finish, shows that women strongly desired to have children, that barrenness was often a curse from God,[83] and that when a barren woman miraculously had a child she rejoiced greatly. Our church culture has drifted far from this standard.

In the Bible, the desire for children is portrayed with earnest longing and deep emotional significance. Sarah, Abraham's wife, was barren for many years. Her distress over her inability to have children is evident in Genesis 16:1-2, where she gave her maidservant Hagar to

---

82 "In our own age, characterized as it is by overpopulation, birth control, and increasingly fragmented families, the biblical portrait of the child as divine blessing may appear quaint to some and even oppressive to others. Nevertheless, it would be unwise to dismiss outright so consistent a testimony; pregnancy is never seen as a curse, nor children as divine punishment for sexual promiscuity." Bruce N. Fisk, "Abortion," in Walter A. Elwell, ed., *Baker Theological Dictionary of the Bible* (Grand Rapids: Baker, 1996), 3.

83 e.g., Gen. 20:18; 2 Sam. 6:20-23; Hos. 9:10-14. Contrast this with the blessing in Gen. 49:25; Exod. 1:20-21; 23:26; Deut. 28:11; Ps. 113:9.

A Child-Friendly and Mother-Supportive Church

Abraham in hopes of building a family through her—a decision, however, that led to further complications and sorrow.

Isaac's wife, Rebekah, was barren for many years. Isaac prayed to the Lord on her behalf, and she soon conceived and gave birth to twins, Esau and Jacob (Gen. 25:21). Their conception and birth were God's blessing in answer to their prayers.

Rachel, Jacob's favorite wife, was deeply distressed by her barrenness, while her sister Leah bore many children. Rachel's anguish is expressed in Genesis 30:1, where she says to Jacob, "Give me children, or else I die."[84] The anguish of these women shows a biblical worldview that sees children as a precious gift from God, not as an optional choice.

Consider Hannah, who wept bitterly[85] because she was barren, pouring out her soul to the Lord (1 Sam. 1:10). The passage describes her as "greatly distressed" over this. In her prayer, she refers to her situation as one of "affliction" (v. 11).

Consider also the Shunammite woman who showed hospitality to the prophet Elisha. She was childless until Elisha prayed for her, and God miraculously gave her a son as a blessing (2 Kgs. 4:8-17).

Elizabeth, the mother of John the Baptist, was described as being righteous before God but barren in her old age (Luke 1:6-7).[86] Her longing for a child and the joy of her eventual pregnancy are highlighted in the Christmas story, where she expresses how God has taken away her disgrace by granting her a child (vv. 24-25). Luke records Elizabeth's excitement over Mary's pregnancy as well (vv. 39-45), showing that having children is a delightful occasion to be celebrated (cf. v. 58).

Our culture, however, has distorted this biblical view, often portraying children as a hindrance to personal success and fulfillment. This

---

84 Consider also verse 23, where she says, "God has taken away my reproach" when she gives birth to Joseph (cf. Luke 1:24-25).

85 The doubling of the word for "weep" in the Hebrew here emphasizes the intensity of her anguish (cf. 2 Sam. 13:36; Jer. 22:10).

86 Elizabeth's situation proves that being barren is not always a form of discipline from the Lord.

mindset has infiltrated even the Church, leading many young Christian couples to believe that delaying or altogether avoiding having children is an amoral decision, subject to individual preference and Christian liberty. While responsible family planning may have its place, and perhaps not every Christian couple is obligated to have as many children as biologically possible, it is crucial that our attitudes toward procreation are shaped by Scripture rather than societal norms. The key issue is our heart posture—are we viewing children through the lens of Scripture, or are we allowing cultural values of convenience and personal ambition to shape our perspective?

Psalm 127 beautifully expresses God's perspective on children:

Behold, children are a gift of the LORD,
The fruit of the womb is a reward.
Like arrows in the hand of a warrior,
So are the children of one's youth.
How blessed is the man whose quiver is full of them;
They will not be ashamed
When they speak with their enemies in the gate. (Psalm 127:3-5)

Here, children are depicted not as burdens but as blessings, enriching the lives of their parents and contributing to the strength and vitality of the family. It even seems that the Psalmist was not satisfied with having one or two children just so he can say he fulfilled the command to multiply, but rather it seems he wanted as many as he and his wife could conceive. His imagery of a full quiver suggests that he saw great value in having many children, not as a burdensome duty but as a source of strength and legacy.

To reform our thinking, the church should embrace a biblical view of children. Pastors can help by teaching Scripture's perspective on the value of children and the joy they bring, rather than allowing cultural misconceptions to shape the conversation. Church members, especially those in leadership, should model a love for children by speaking positively about parenthood, celebrating births, and supporting families in meaningful ways. This could include offering practical help to struggling single mothers, fostering a strong community for young parents, and providing resources for those navigating the challenges of raising children. There is no cookie cutter solution that every church must follow. Each church will adapt to its own setting based on its members' gifts and the women God brings across its path.[87]

In reorienting our view of children to align with Scripture, we not only honor God's design but also create a church culture that values life at all stages. By embracing a biblical perspective on procreation, we can stand against the tide of abortion and be the light of Christ in a world that devalues children and families. The Church, through its witness and example, has the power to transform society by upholding the truth that every child is a precious gift from God.

Minister to women and children

A prevalent misconception often voiced against pro-life activists is that Christians care only about preventing abortion and neglect the needs of children and mothers afterward, as if their involvement ends once another abortion is avoided. This misconception that Christians don't care about children after birth arises largely from a narrow focus on their pro-life advocacy, missing the broader picture of all the other ways a church ministers to women and children. However, this critique does bring up a good point—if we advocate for the protection of the preborn but fail to support mothers in need, our witness is compromised and we become hypocrites.[88]

God's people must be generous people

God has always commanded His people to care for the poor and has always forbidden them from harming the poor. For example, in Deuteronomy 27, God issues a stern warning against injustice or inflicting harm on the needy: "Cursed is he who distorts the justice due an alien, orphan, and widow" (v. 19). In Exodus 22:21-24, God warns

---

87 See the "Lessons for Pro-Life Pastors" in Justin Taylor, "Abortion Is About God," in Sam Storms and Justin Taylor, eds., *For the Fame of God's Name: Essays in Honor of John Piper* (Wheaton: Crossway, 2010), 342–49.

88 See the "Call to Action" in Stott, *Issues Facing Christians Today*, 407–9.

against afflicting strangers, widows, and orphans, declaring that if they cry out, He will hear their plea and act on their behalf (cf. vv. 25-27; Lev. 25:35-38; Deut. 24:14-15; Ps. 12:5; Prov. 22:22-23; Jas. 5:4).[89]

The Bible regularly commands believers to show compassion to orphans and widows.[90] It might seem out of place to use these texts as a means of promoting pro-life activism. However, the point of these passages is not that orphans and widows are the only people we are allowed to help—the point is to protect *all* who are defenseless! An "orphan" is only a hop, skip and a jump from a preborn baby whose father is pressuring their mother to abort them. In the same way, a "widow" is not far removed from a pregnant woman whose boyfriend or husband is out of the picture. This is not an attempt to stretch the applicability of Scripture. This is an affirmation that the same God who upheld the cause of the orphans continues to value and protect defenseless children today.[91]

Compassion in the Law (...of Christ)

These principles were applied in specific commands regarding care for the poor—whether through the Sabbath year (Exod. 23:10-11), regulations on harvesting (Lev. 19:9-10; 23:22; Deut. 24:19-21), as well as rules about finances (Lev. 25:35-38; Deut. 14:28-29; 26:12). All of these would ensure that the poor among Israel were taken care of.

These commands to care for the needy among them are sometimes rooted in their own history as slaves and foreigners in Egypt. The Lord

---

89 The Lord promises that He will arise to defend the needy. He is a God who delivers the afflicted, a divine protector who hears their cries and intervenes on their behalf (Ps. 35:10; Jer. 20:13). The Lord is a refuge and defense for the oppressed, providing shelter and safety from harm (Isa. 25:4). He exalts the needy to a high and secure place where no adversary can reach them (Ps. 107:41). Standing at their right hand, He maintains their cause and champions their rights (Deut. 10:18; Pss. 109:31; 140:12). He raises up, loves, protects, and supports the downtrodden (Ps. 146:8-9).

90 Exod. 22:22; Deut. 14:29; 24:17; Ps. 82:3; Isa. 1:17; Jas. 1:27.

91 How can a preborn child not fall under the umbrella of the "weak" (Ps. 82:3-4), the "needy" (Exod. 23:6; Prov. 31:9; Isa. 25:4), or the "afflicted" (Job 36:6, 15; Ps. 140:12), whom we are also called to minister to?

A Child-Friendly and Mother-Supportive Church

commands, "You shall not wrong a stranger or oppress him, *for* you were strangers in the land of Egypt" (Exod. 22:21, emphasis mine). This concern is repeated in Exodus 23:9, where God reminds them not to oppress a stranger specifically *because* they themselves know the pain of oppression (cf. Lev. 19:33-34; Deut. 10:19; 24:17-22).

Moving into the New Testament, Jesus' sacrifice has given us the perfect model for how to love one another, and we are to show others the same love we experienced in Christ. Believers are repeatedly called to imitate God by walking in love and forgiving one another, just as Christ has loved and forgiven us (Eph. 4:32-5:2; Col. 3:12-13; cf. Rom. 15:7). Having been redeemed by God's free, unmerited grace, we cannot help but show the same grace and mercy to others.

In Luke 6:36, Jesus commands, "Be merciful, just as your Father is merciful." This is not merely a command to refrain from retaliation or to overlook offenses. The surrounding context emphasizes doing good, lending, and giving to those who cannot repay us, those who are ungrateful, and even our enemies (vv. 27-36). Being merciful, then, involves more than refraining from vengeance; it means actively doing good toward others in the name of Jesus.

These New Testament teachings remind us that our acts of compassion reflect God's mercy to us in Christ. He took pity on us when we were dead in sin as His compassion moved Him to rescue us. As we have been shown mercy in our helpless estate, we are called to be vessels of that same mercy, extending compassion to the afflicted and needy. Our lives should be marked by tangible acts of kindness, generosity, and justice. In doing so, we fulfill the law of Christ and embody the heart of the gospel, making God's compassion visible to a watching world that devalues the preborn and destroys women's lives.

As we have seen, the gospel reaches into every aspect of our lives, including how we view and support children and mothers within the church. The gospel calls us to purity and holiness, transforming our

83

hearts so that we resist temptations for premarital sex and avoid the anxieties it brings. It renews our minds, helping us to see children as blessings rather than burdens, and it compels us to be generous and supportive to those in need.

When a church embraces these gospel-driven principles, the members offer eternal hope and practical help to mothers facing the daunting task of raising children. Through the love and support of the church, fear and anxiety can be replaced with trust in God's provision, ensuring that no mother faces the challenges of raising a child alone.

–8–

Politicians Must Abolish and Criminalize Abortion

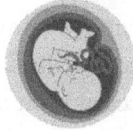

T hroughout biblical history, the prophets of Israel did not remain silent in the face of injustice. They boldly confronted the leaders of their day, demanding justice for all. Their voices rang out with the urgency of God's authority, calling kings and rulers to account for their actions while exhorting them to defend the oppressed and protect the innocent.

Today, as we face the grave issue of abortion, the prophetic tradition compels us to raise our voices as well. The preborn—the most vulnerable and voiceless among us—are being led to slaughter. It is our solemn duty, as followers of Christ and as citizens, to call upon our leaders to uphold justice, defend the defenseless, and end this modern-day atrocity.

Isaiah, Jeremiah, Ezekiel, and others provide powerful examples of courageous preaching. They did not shy away from rebuking the rulers of their time for shedding innocent blood and neglecting the needs of the poor and oppressed, even at the risk of their own lives. They spoke with God's authority, urging repentance and a return to His standards of justice.

In this chapter, we will explore how these prophets challenged their leaders and how their example guides us in our present struggle to protect the preborn. We will see that it is not only appropriate but imperative for Christians to engage with political leaders, urging them to fulfill their God-given responsibility to safeguard the innocent.[92]

Isaiah's message to pro-choice politicians

Isaiah's prophetic ministry includes stern rebukes to rulers and leaders who perpetuate injustice and shed innocent blood. His words challenge us today to hold our leaders accountable for protecting the innocent and vulnerable, including the preborn.

In Isaiah 1, the prophet delivers a scathing indictment against unjust rulers, likening them to the infamous immoral cities of Sodom and Gomorrah (v. 10).[93] In calling them by these names, God is declaring that Israel's leaders, through their corruption and neglect of justice, are just as wicked as those ancient cities.

What is particularly striking is that Isaiah addresses those who are outwardly religious. Despite their celebrations of holy days, their prayers, their worship, and their sacrifices (vv. 12-14), God is repulsed by their hypocrisy. Their religious observances are meaningless because they neglect the poor and fail to do justice (vv. 15-17, 23).

Isaiah's message intensifies in chapter 3, where the Lord contends with the rulers of His people.

The LORD arises to contend,
And stands to judge the people.
The LORD enters into judgment with the elders
　　and princes of His people,
"It is you who have devoured the vineyard;

92　It cannot be argued that, since the prophets spoke to a nation in covenant relation to God, these warnings are not applicable to all nations as well. God frequently expresses His anger toward pagan nations for practicing child sacrifice (Deut. 18:9-14; 2 Kgs. 16:3; 21:2-9), and they are accountable under His Law (Rom. 2:14-15; 3:19-20; Gal. 3:10-14; 1 Tim. 1:8-11).
93　The reference to Sodom is "a symbol of sin paraded, sin as an accepted life-style" (Motyer, *Isaiah*, 46).

The plunder of the poor is in your houses.
What do you mean by crushing My people
And grinding the face of the poor?"
Declares the Lord GOD of hosts. (Isaiah 3:13-15)

These leaders are condemned for their exploitation of the poor. Isaiah describes how they plunder the poor, crushing and grinding them in their oppression.[94] This vivid imagery shows the severity of their actions and the depth of their sin.

Chapter 10 brings another powerful rebuke. Here, God pronounces "woe" upon those who "enact evil statutes" (v. 1). This includes any law that permits the harm or exploitation of orphans and widows (vv. 2-3). While legalized abortion was not the particular evil statute Isaiah had in mind, it clearly falls under the same condemnation. Just as these leaders' neglect and exploitation harmed the poor, so too does the legal sanctioning of abortion destroy the most vulnerable lives under the guise of choice and convenience. Legalized abortion, along with all pro-choice legislation, is an evil statute.

The prophet warns of a coming "day of punishment" and a time of "devastation" for those who perpetuate such evil (v. 3). Politicians who fail to protect the preborn will likewise face God's righteous judgment.

As Christians, we too have the duty and privilege of calling our leaders back to the biblical standard and urging them to protect the most vulnerable. Pro-life activism cannot be dismissed as "too political for church." Just as Isaiah confronted the leaders of his day, we too must call upon our own political leaders to fulfill their duty to do justice and show mercy.

Jeremiah's and Ezekiel's cry for justice

Jeremiah and Ezekiel stand as towering prophetic figures who boldly called upon the leaders of their time to enact justice and protect the oppressed.

---

94 "The poetic parallel [of 'crushing' and 'grinding'] indicates both a sense of violence and debasement" (W. R. Domeris, "דכא," in *NIDOTTE* 1:944). cf. Ps. 94:5; Prov. 22:22-23.

Thinking Biblically About Abortion

In Jeremiah 22, the oracle is directed to the king of Judah and his associates (vv. 1-2). The prophet commands them to do justice and righteousness, to deliver the oppressed, and to refrain from mistreating the orphan and widow or shedding innocent blood (v. 3). Jeremiah delivers a clear message: there is a promise of reward for those who obey these commands (v. 4) and a severe warning for those who do not (v. 5). The prophet pronounces woe upon those who withhold wages (v. 13), or who seek dishonest gain, shed innocent blood, and oppress others (v. 17). He proclaims that, instead of permitting this evil to continue, it is a king's duty to execute justice and righteousness (v. 15) and to plead the cause of the afflicted and needy (v. 16).

Ezekiel continues this prophetic tradition of rebuking unjust rulers. In Ezekiel 22, God, through the prophet, condemns the leaders for their bloodshed and oppression:

> Behold, the rulers of Israel, each according to his power, have been in you for the purpose of shedding blood. They have treated father and mother lightly within you. The alien they have oppressed in your midst; the fatherless and the widow they have wronged in you. (Ezekiel 22:6-7)

They have wronged the needy, the widows, the orphans, and the aliens. Ezekiel's indictment is severe, highlighting the moral and spiritual failures of the leaders who were meant to protect the vulnerable.

Both Jeremiah and Ezekiel serve as powerful reminders of the biblical call to justice. They challenge us to hold our leaders accountable for the protection of the innocent and the oppressed. The preborn, who are the most defenseless among us, fall squarely into this category. We are called to advocate for laws and policies that uphold the sanctity of life and to speak out against any form of oppression or injustice. Just as these prophets condemned the shedding of innocent blood in their time, we must recognize that abortion is the modern equivalent—the legalized destruction of the most helpless members of society.

The prophetic tradition, therefore, demands that we not remain silent in the face of injustice. We are called to act, to speak out, and to hold our leaders accountable.

Good kings end child sacrifice

Throughout the history of Israel, we see that when kings heeded the words of the prophets and turned back to the Lord, their righteous actions often included tearing down high places and abolishing practices such as child sacrifice. This biblical precedent highlights the responsibility and authority of political leaders to end practices that are abhorrent to God, including modern-day equivalents like abortion. Like the child sacrifices performed in ancient Israel, abortion is a horrific practice in which innocent lives are taken, often justified by cultural norms or personal convenience. Abolishing injustices like abortion is not outside their realm; rather, it is their God-given duty to uphold justice and righteousness.

Consider the example of King Josiah. His revival, detailed in 2 Kings 23, demonstrates his commitment to the Lord by putting an end to the practice of child sacrifice. Verse 10 specifically notes that he "defiled Topheth ... that no man might make his son or his daughter pass through the fire for Molech."[95] Notice how Josiah's actions were a direct response to reading the Word and the prophetic call to righteousness (cf. 22:8f).

Similarly, King Asa, upon repenting, removed idols from the land. He "removed the foreign altars and high places, tore down the sacred pillars, [and] cut down the Asherim" (2 Chr. 14:3). King Asa also commanded the people to serve the Lord, reinforcing his leadership in guiding the nation back to true worship (v. 4; cf. 15:8-15). Like Josiah's, his reforms as well were in response to prophetic preaching (15:1-7).

---

95 The specification of these several false deities shows how the reform under Josiah was "comprehensive and thorough" (Iain W. Provan, *1 & 2 Kings*, Understanding the Bible Commentary Series [Grand Rapids: Baker, 2012], 273).

Thinking Biblically About Abortion

Hezekiah, another exemplary king, "removed the high places and broke down the sacred pillars and cut down the Asherah" (2 Kgs. 18:4). His actions were a clear stand against idolatry and a move toward restoring proper worship in Judah.[96] Jehoshaphat also took significant steps in this direction, tearing down the high places and seeking to lead the people in following the Lord (2 Chr. 17:6; 19:3).

In several instances, Scripture records that while certain kings did what was right in the eyes of the Lord, one major fault of theirs was allowing the high places to remain.[97] This indicates that God desired a more thorough reformation, one that included the removal of all practices contrary to His commands. The persistent mention of the high places signifies that complete obedience to God requires eliminating all forms of idolatry and child sacrifice.

These historical accounts strongly support the biblical truth that it is righteous for political leaders to take decisive action against practices that violate the sanctity of life. It is not a matter of mixing religion and politics. The duty to protect the innocent, including the preborn, is a sacred responsibility that leaders are called to uphold.

In our time, the church's public proclamation to end abortion is a continuation of the prophetic tradition to stand against practices that devalue human life. Political leaders today have the authority and obligation to pass laws that protect the most vulnerable, just as the kings of Israel did. Their ancient example is a powerful reminder for leaders today that true leadership involves courageous obedience to Christ.

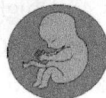

Isaiah's denunciation of unjust rulers, Jeremiah's call to do justice and righteousness, and Ezekiel's rebuke of those who shed innocent blood serve as timeless reminders of our duty to defend the oppressed. These

---

96 Consider also Hezekiah's repentance in response to Micah's preaching (Jer. 26:18-19; Mic. 3:12).
97 Johoash (2 Kgs. 12:3), Amaziah (14:4), Jotham (15:35), Asa (2 Chr. 15:17), Jehoshaphat (20:33).

prophets did not merely critique; they called for action, for leaders to turn from their wicked ways and to embrace the ways of the Lord.

In the same vein, we are called to be prophetic voices in our generation, advocating for the most vulnerable among us—the preborn. This is not merely a political issue; it is a moral imperative grounded in Scripture. As we have seen through the examples of godly kings like Josiah, Asa, Hezekiah, and Jehoshaphat, it is within the realm of righteous leadership to abolish practices that are abhorrent to God, including the modern atrocity of abortion.

Let us, therefore, commit to being voices for the voiceless, to challenging our leaders to enact just laws that protect the innocent, and to standing firm in the truth that every life is precious in the sight of God.[98]

---

98   Given how often the Bible speaks of being under the Law as bondage and salvation as freedom from the Law (Rom. 7:1-4; 1 Cor. 9:19-23; 2 Cor. 3:4-11; Gal. 4:4-5), and with its explicit declarations that the Law is abolished (Eph. 2:14-15; Col. 2:16-17; Heb. 7:11-22; 8:7-13; 10:9), it does not go as far as the theonomists hope in advocating for the legislature of the entire Mosaic Law. In many of the passages explored in this chapter, the Law was reestablished in Israel because the Old Covenant was in place at that time. That said, however, any Christian would agree that, regardless of whether a nation is in covenant with God, they should establish laws protecting the innocent against violence, as in the case of abortion.

- Epilogue -

Can a Christian Be Pro-Choice?

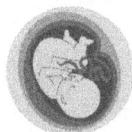

G iven the overwhelming biblical evidence for the sanctity of human life presented in this book, a pressing question remains: why is there division in the church over the issue of abortion? Is this a matter where we can simply agree to disagree? Many sincere Christians struggle with this topic, either due to cultural influence, personal experiences, or misunderstandings of Scripture. But as followers of Christ, our ultimate standard must be God's Word, not personal preference or societal norms. What about the individual who claims to follow Christ while also embracing a pro-choice position? Can a believer disregard the Scriptures that affirm the sanctity of life? And is it sinful to deny the personhood and rights of the preborn?

Christians must embrace the *whole* Bible

We will all be judged based on what we know. Certainly a new believer has a grace period to grow out of their secular thinking. We can't expect them to have perfect doctrine if they have not even read through the Bible yet. However, in their daily devotions it won't be long before they come across a passage relevant to the pro-life issue. Then, if their conversion was true, and if they really do trust God and wish to conform their thinking to Christ's, they will soon become pro-life.

However, this question of being a pro-choice Christian is most often asked not by new believers, but by those who know better, and yet wish to keep one foot in the world and one foot in the church. This same tension arises in many doctrinal debates—Christian evolutionism, Christian feminism, Christian psychology—but nowhere is it more urgent than in the issue of life and death. The attitude is that so long as one believes the basics of the faith, it doesn't matter what else they may believe about "secondary" or "tertiary" issues. This mindset proposes that so long as one believes that Jesus died and rose again then they are in the clear, as if God is only concerned about getting people into heaven but not how they live as Christians. This same compromise is evident in the abortion debate, where some professing Christians attempt to justify their pro-choice stance despite clear biblical teaching on the sanctity of life.

But while it is true that the death, burial, and resurrection of Christ is the central message of the gospel (1 Cor. 15:3f), and while Paul's focus when planting churches was "Christ, and Him crucified" (1 Cor. 2:2), yet at the same time, Jesus and His apostles show strong concern for obedience as well. In the New Testament we see that disagreements on *moral* issues are labeled heresy, and sound doctrine includes accuracy in matters of orthopraxy as well as orthodoxy regarding the person and work of Christ.

Consider how Paul views right practice as part of sound doctrine. Paul exhorts Titus to instruct men and women, young and old, regarding family order and gender roles, calling it "sound doctrine" (Titus 2:1f). First Timothy 1:8-11 contains one of Paul's many vice lists, which mentions "murderers" (which would include all who participate in abortions). At the conclusion, he admits his intention was not to be exhaustive by adding, "and whatever else is contrary to *sound teaching*," (v. 10, emphasis mine), which is part of "the glorious gospel" (v. 11). In 1 Timothy 6:3 and Titus 1:1, Paul speaks of doctrine *according to godliness*, thus lumping moral teaching in with orthodoxy. This shows that an understanding of right and wrong—including the sinfulness of abortion —is basic Christian teaching.

Beyond that, take a look at how Paul viewed those who disagree with core Christian teaching on moral issues. In 1 Thessalonians 4, after a lengthy exhortation to "abstain from sexual immorality" (v. 3f), Paul says that whoever rejects this teaching is not rejecting him, but God (v. 8). In fact, he rebukes those who disagree with his moral teachings as "conceited" and "understand[ing] nothing" (1 Tim. 6:4).[99]

In the Great Commission, part of discipling the nations is to teach them *everything* that Jesus taught (Matt. 28:20). This includes His teachings about murder (Matt. 5:21-26), about how our murderous thoughts come from our sin nature and defile us (Matt. 15:15-20), about how Satan has been a murderer from the beginning (John 8:42-47), about how little children are precious to Jesus (Matt. 18:1-6), and about how we must love our (pregnant and preborn) neighbor as ourselves (Matt. 22:36-40).

We find, therefore, abundant testimony to how not only the person and work of Christ is an essential of the faith, but beliefs about Christian practice as well.

A Christian's attitude toward God's Word

There is a connection between our hearts and our minds. Heresy becomes a heart issue as it reveals our discontent with God's moral standards, preferring our own. If we as "Christians" trust the testimony found in God's Word regarding His Son, and yet we despise—or worse, *detest*—what the Word says about any other matter of doctrine and practice, then something is off balance in our understanding of God's Word.

---

99 Paul even critiques those who contend against a practice as "tertiary" as head coverings (1 Cor. 11:16)! Consider also his attitude toward those who resist his requirement for women to be silent in churches, calling such objectors unspiritual and unrecognized (1 Cor. 14:34-38).

Thinking Biblically About Abortion

Some who struggle with this issue may have personal pain—whether past abortions, pressure from loved ones, or fear of what embracing the truth might require of them. But God's grace is abundant, and He calls us not to justify sin, but to turn to Him for forgiveness and reconciliation through Christ. We should embrace the truth wholeheartedly rather than allowing our past to cloud our judgment, or worse, twist Scripture to justify sin.

Most, if not all, of the objections to the biblical pro-life position boil down to either:

- "I don't like it,"
- "I will do whatever I want,"
- "My autonomy trumps God's will for me," or,
- "A fetus is not a child," which amounts to a denial of basic biology and anthropology, both of which line up with God's own testimony in Scripture.

These are not the attitudes of a Spirit-filled follower of Jesus Christ!

Consider also what one is condoning if they are pro-choice. They are allowing the mass slaughter of innocent little children to happen right in their own backyard. They are perpetuating a second Holocaust that has cost at least ten times as many lives as the first one. They are allowing women to be pressured into making a decision that will haunt them the rest of their lives. They are harming women physically, emotionally, and spiritually.

Even if one is not actively lobbying for pro-choice legislation, their idleness gives women the impression that the Church can't help them, and their silence leaves these women without hope. Remember, blood is on our hands even by neglecting the needs of the oppressed (Isa. 1). Even if one has never had an abortion or funded an abortion, they are not necessarily off the hook. In Romans 1:32, Paul condemns those who even *give approval* to ungodly practices! Just because he didn't physically stone him, Paul wasn't innocent of Stephen's blood when he gave hearty approval to his execution (Acts 8:1), was he?

Can a Christian Be Pro-Choice?

But again we can get at the heart of the issue by asking *why* the person disagrees with God's instructions about protecting life. In reality, the debate is rarely about a lack of biblical clarity but rather about a refusal to submit to God's authority on this issue. Is it merely because the passages are confusing or ambiguous? If clarity was brought to those texts, would the person be willing to submit to whatever God says? We could extend grace to somebody still wrestling with the issue. However, usually the attitude is more that the biblical authors were Neanderthals and knew nothing of fetal development (despite the fact that modern science agrees 100% with the biblical data). One can pay lip service to the sixth commandment, but then usurp the authority to decide when exceptions can be made. Or in the worst of cases, one will admit that the fetus is a human, admit that abortion is murder, and yet still feel it is their (or a woman's) right to abort them. That is not biblical Christianity.

- Appendix -

Exodus 21:22-25
Problem Text or
Proof Text?

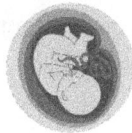

T his passage has become a subject of heated debate, seemingly offering contrasting meanings at first glance.[100] Proponents of the pro-choice stance have often cited this as evidence that an unborn baby holds less significance than an adult human life. They interpret this text to imply that the mother is safeguarded by *lex talionis* while the unborn child is not. Yet, upon careful examination, such an interpretation is impossible. It is astonishing how this misinter-

---

100 See also H. Wayne House, "Miscarriage Or Premature Birth: Additional Thoughts on Exodus 21:22-25," in *Westminster Theological Journal* 41.1 (1978); Hoffmeier, *Abortion*, 57–61; Davis, *Abortion and the Christian*, 49–52; Grudem, *What the Bible Says*, 14–18; John S. Feinberg and Paul D. Feinberg, *Ethics for a Brave New World* (Wheaton: Crossway, 1993), 63–65.

Thinking Biblically About Abortion

pretation gained traction despite its inconsistency with a fair rendering of the original Hebrew.[101]

The text reads:

> If men struggle with each other and strike a woman with child so that she gives birth prematurely, yet there is no injury, he shall surely be fined as the woman's husband may demand of him, and he shall pay as the judges decide. But if there is any further[102] injury, then you shall appoint as a penalty life for life, eye for eye, tooth for tooth, hand for hand, foot for foot, burn for burn, wound for wound, bruise for bruise. (Exodus 21:22-25)

According to the pro-choice reading, the pregnant woman gets too close to a scuffle and suffers a blow to the abdomen, resulting in a mis-carriage—not a premature birth. Thus, their argument contends that since the penalty imposed on the man responsible is merely a fine for the inconvenience caused, the miscarried baby must not be considered human. They suggest that if any further harm befalls the woman *alone*, then the law of retaliation is enacted, implying a protection under law for the mother that is not present for the child.[103]

---

101 It is far from true that this passage is "not clear" (R. A. Higginson, "Ethics of Medical Care," in David J. Atkinson and David F. Field, eds., *New Dictionary of Christian Ethics and Pastoral Theology* [Downers Grove: InterVarsity, 1995], 93) or "exegetically ambiguous" (E. D. Cook, "Abortion," *ibid.*, 133).

102 The words "any further" are absent from the Hebrew and may inadver-tently make the passage sound more pro-choice. This insertion changes the meaning from, "If any harm was caused to the woman or her child," to "If any harm was caused to the woman beyond her miscarriage." How-ever, a literal rendering of the Hebrew would simply be: "If mischief occurs," without favoritism shown to the mother. See also House, "Mis-carriage," 118.

103 Even if one interprets this as a miscarriage, it does not necessarily imply that the preborn are not individual human beings or that abortion is per-missible. See R. Alan Cole, *Exodus: An Introduction and Commentary*, Tyndale Old Testament Commentaries (Downers Grove: InterVarsity, 1977), 169; Ronald J. Sider, *Completely Pro-Life: Building a Consistent Stance on Abortion, the Family, Nuclear Weapons, the Poor* (Eugene: Wipf and Stock, 1987), 46–47.

Exodus 21:22-25 - Problem Text or Proof Text?

So, basically, a miscarried child who loses their life does not receive justice through the perpetrator repaying life for life, according to this rather forced interpretation. This take on the passage tries to avoid the implication that the prematurely born child, if harmed, is protected under law.

As we delve deeper into the language and context of the passage, it becomes clear that such a pro-choice interpretation lacks justification.[104]

The crux of the debate centers on a clause in verse 22, which receives various renderings. Some translations depict it as something along the lines of, "she gives birth prematurely," aligning with a more pro-life interpretation. Others convey it as "she has a miscarriage" or something similar, which favors the pro-choice viewpoint—even if unintentionally. Meanwhile, some translations maintain a neutral stance, closely mirroring the original text by stating something akin to "her children come out of her."

The phrase in question is literally: "her children go out." That's all it says. Nothing more; nothing less.

To discern the unfolding events in this legal scenario, we must dissect the significance of the terms "children" and "goes out." Both these words, when understood properly, teach the markedly pro-life essence of this passage.

Firstly, the specific term for "child[ren]" in Scripture frequently signifies one's children or descendants. Hence, what emerges from this woman is not an indistinct mass, a nebulous blob, a parasite, or a donkey—it is her child, her offspring, her baby. Why there is any debate on this issue, since the word means "child" and nothing else, I cannot comprehend.

Next is the word meaning "go out" or "depart." This word appears frequently in the Old Testament across diverse contexts, but specific to our discussion, the word often indicates the act of giving birth.[105] Since

---

104 A concise but helpful summary of the details can be found in Fisk, "Abortion," 4.

105 cf. Gen. 25:25-26; 38:27-30; 2 Chr. 32:21; Jer. 1:5; 20:18.

the context in Exodus 21 involves a pregnant woman, a straightforward reading of this verse suggests a live birth.

Pro-choice interpreters may argue that the word "go out" is sometimes linked with passages referring to a miscarriage, citing Numbers 12:12 and Job 3:11.

Oh, do not let her be like one dead, whose flesh is half eaten away when he comes from his mother's womb! (Num. 12:12)

Why did I not die at birth,
Come forth from the womb and expire? (Job 3:11)

However, in both these instances, the presence of the word for death or dying gives the meaning of a miscarriage. Consequently, the Hebrew term for "going out" in those verses does not mean "miscarriage" in and of itself, but rather, only when connected with "death," does the term indicate that the baby goes out *dead*. These two passages cannot imply that the Hebrew word for "go out" universally means "miscarriage."

Context is key. Where the surrounding verses explicitly give additional clues implying a stillbirth or miscarriage, we may interpret it as such. However, in the absence of any such indication, we should assume the birth was to a healthy baby.

Regardless, these passages inherently support a pro-life stance! Job 3 has already been examined in an earlier chapter and was proven to be a powerful pro-life proof text. In Numbers 12:12, the reference to what lies within the womb possessing flesh unequivocally signifies human flesh. "Flesh" signifies vitality and growth in a typical pregnancy. Moreover, the personal pronoun "he" and the possessive pronouns "his," and "whose," assign personhood to this fleshly being. The term "dead" doesn't portray the child as an inanimate object but as someone who was once alive.

Exodus 21:22-25 - Problem Text or Proof Text?

Far from proving that the Hebrew term for "go out" universally (or *ever*) means miscarriage,[106] Numbers 12:12 and Job 3:11 reinforce the biblical affirmation of human life within the womb. They also demonstrate that when the biblical writers intended to convey a miscarriage, they provided specific contextual clues.

Further supporting this is the existence of separate Hebrew words for miscarriage[107] and untimely birth,[108] either of which Moses could have utilized in Exodus 21:22-25 had that been the intended meaning.[109]

Another crucial aspect to consider is the significance of Moses' highlighting of the woman's pregnancy in this scenario. If the sole intention were to establish equitable laws like "eye for eye" or "tooth for tooth," there would be no need to mention a pregnant woman or her situation. The text draws attention to her pregnancy, implying its relevance within the legal context. It suggests that the developing child in

---

106 Ps. 144:14 is the one text where this Hebrew word for "goes out" is sometimes understood as a reference to a miscarriage (compare ESV with NIV). Some interpret the oxen "bearing" as bearing offspring and the "going out" to mean that the cattle's pregnancies are healthy and without miscarriage (cf. Gen. 31:38). However, this is an untenable translation. First, the word for "bearing" here is never used for pregnancy or bearing children but instead means to carry a load, bear a burden, and, by extension, toil or forced labor—something fitting for oxen. Second, the word for "mishap" literally refers to a breach, usually in a wall, so it seems that the word it is paired with—which again is the common word for "going out" in some fashion—would carry that same nuance. The meaning of the verse, therefore, is better understood as saying that the oxen will be strong in v. 14a, and then the topic of livestock is dropped in v. 14b as the psalmist shifts focus to humanity. He desires that the walls of the city would protect the people so that no enemies would get in and no citizens would be carried out into captivity (cf. Amos 4:3). See also Goldingay *Psalms*, vol. 3, 689–90. "It is used of going forth from one's homeland into exile (Ps. 114:14)" (Warren Baker and Eugene Carpenter, eds., *The Complete Word Study Dictionary: Old Testament* [Chattanooga: AMG, 2003], 462).

107 e.g., Gen. 31:38; Exod. 23:26; Job 21:10.

108 e.g., Job 3:16; Ps. 58:8; Eccl. 6:3.

109 House, "Miscarriage," 111.

her womb is significant to this case law. Otherwise, there would be no logical reason to reference her condition; the fact that the men struck a woman would suffice.

Moreover, this interpretation seems remarkably insensitive. The alternate scenario suggests that if an injury results in a miscarriage, it warrants only a fine, while any other harm demands a more severe response. Picture someone minimizing the woman's pain, casually saying, "You had a miscarriage, but hey, at least you didn't lose a tooth!" Such an interpretation lacks empathy and fails to grasp the profound emotional and physical toll of losing a child.

This analysis challenges interpretations of the case law in Exodus 21 that undermine the sanctity of the unborn. The careful examination of language and context reinforces the inherent value of the unborn child and highlights the importance of considering harm done to the child in legal contexts. These insights affirm the pro-life understanding of the sanctity and dignity of human life from its earliest stages. Developing children in the womb must be protected by law.[110]

---

110 I cannot agree more with Montgomery's conclusion: "To interpret the passage in any other way is to strain the text intolerably, and efforts at emendation ... are neither necessary nor helpful" (*Slaughter of the Innocents*, 101).

Scripture Index

Scripture Index

Scripture Index

11:4	69	7:6	73	31:27	43
13:16	32	7:30-31	50, 64	32:35	50, 60, 61
15:5	71	7:32-34	64	32:43	43
25:4	82	7:30	50	33:10	43
29:16	22	7:31	61	33:12	43
33:11	34	7:32-34	64	36:29	43
42:6	69	9:21	32	44:7	32
43:1	25	11:20	19, 68, 69	44:26	55
43:7	25	12:2	19	49:13	55
43:21	25	15:1-4	65	50:3	43
44:2	25	17:9	11	51:54	71
44:21	25	17:10	19, 68	51:62	43
44:24	25	18:22	71		
45:13	69	19:4-5	65	**Lamentations**	
45:23	55	19:5	61	1:5	32
46:3	25	20:12	19	2:11	32
46:3-4	21	20:13	82	2:20	32
46:13	69	20:14-18	32	3:58	71, 72
48:8	25	20:17	32	4:4	32
49:1	25, 29	20:18	101		
49:5	25, 29	21:6	43	**Ezekiel**	
49:25	71	22:1-2	88	3:18-20	53
50:8	69	22:3	54, 55, 73	14:21	43
51:1	69	22:4	88	15:4	61
51:22	72	22:5	55, 88	15:6	61
59:4	34	22:10	79	16:20	62
59:7	56	22:13	54, 55, 73,	16:20-21	62
59:13	34		88	16:22	50
62:8	55	22:15	88	20:3	63
		22:16	72, 88	20:25-32	60
Jeremiah		22:17	54, 88	20:26	50, 63
1:5	20, 25, 101	26:18-19	90	20:27	61
5:28	69, 71	27:5	43	20:30-31	61
6:11	32				

111

Scripture Index

8:7-13 91
10:9 91
12:9 19
13:2 77
13:4 75
13:5 77

James
1:15 34
1:27 82
1:27-28 72
3:7 41
3:9 38
5:1-6 54
5:4 82

1 Peter
4:9 77

2 Peter
2:12 42

1 John
1:9 13

Jude
1:10 42

Revelation
22:6 19

www.ingramcontent.com/pod-product-compliance
Lightning Source LLC
Chambersburg PA
CBHW061749020426
42331CB00006B/1404